A Patient's Guide to
PSYCHOTHERAPY

A Patient's Guide *to*

PSYCHOTHERAPY

and an Overview for Students and Beginning Therapists

DONALD B. COLSON, PH.D.

A PATIENT'S GUIDE TO PSYCHOTHERAPY
AND AN OVERVIEW FOR STUDENTS AND BEGINNING THERAPISTS

iUniverse books may be ordered through booksellers or by contacting:

iUniverse
1663 Liberty Drive
Bloomington, IN 47403
www.iuniverse.com
1-800-Authors (1-800-288-4677)

Because of the dynamic nature of the Internet, any web addresses or links contained in this book may have changed since publication and may no longer be valid. The views expressed in this work are solely those of the author and do not necessarily reflect the views of the publisher, and the publisher hereby disclaims any responsibility for them.

Any people depicted in stock imagery provided by Thinkstock are models, and such images are being used for illustrative purposes only.
Certain stock imagery © Thinkstock.

ISBN: 978-1-4917-9211-7 (sc)
ISBN: 978-1-4917-9212-4 (e)

Library of Congress Control Number: 2016904207

Print information available on the last page.

iUniverse rev. date: 04/13/2016

CONTENTS

PREFACE

Often in the initial stage of my work with new patients I wished that I had something in writing to explain the therapy process. My opinion is that there is too little attention to providing education for our patients. I am now writing to help fill that gap by explaining therapy to patients, what is involved and what to expect from therapy. I will also be pleased if beginning students of psychotherapy, those in graduate schools, training programs, psychiatric residencies find this text instructive. My experiences doing psychotherapy, teaching and conducting research have reinforced my view of the need for such a text. Perhaps a bit about my background will help to better understand the source of this interest and my qualifications for writing about the subject.

When in 1965 I began post-doctoral training in clinical psychology at The Menninger Clinic (TMC) I had little idea about how influential that training would be. While there I honed skills in psychotherapy and diagnosis and became sure that I wanted to pursue training as a psychoanalyst. I studied with some very accomplished psychoanalysts whom I came to admire for their use of psychoanalytic thinking to understand people. The training helped me discover a path to practice the most extensive and intensive form of psychotherapy, namely psychoanalysis. I learned the application of psychoanalytic knowledge not only to individual psychotherapy but also to group psychotherapy, residential treatment, consultation, supervision, diagnosis and teaching. Conducting psychotherapy was, for me, immeasurably enhanced by psychoanalytic training. Over the years I have supervised and taught psychiatrists, psychologists, social workers and others, all made possible by my occupying various positions in the Menninger School of psychiatry and psychology postdoctoral training program. I did become a psychoanalyst and later was appointed by The American Psychoanalytic Association as a supervising and training analyst which involved training others to become analysts. I was awarded honorary positions at Menninger to support teaching and research. I developed and administered a psychoanalytic psychotherapy training program which still thrives. I became a fellow of The American Group Psychotherapy Association. Also at Menninger I served as Director of Psychology with administrative responsibility for more than 25 psychologists. As part of my academic work I coauthored one book and published over forty articles in professional journals.

INTRODUCTION

Most people in therapy will be satisfied to obtain relief from suffering and improved self-esteem. However, some will also want to delve into how therapy works. I write this book primarily for people already in or considering psychotherapy. Perhaps some others, like a family member, might like to understand the process. The book may also be of interest secondarily to various student groups as an overview of psychotherapy: graduate students in mental health areas, in psychotherapy training programs and study groups. For the readership of experienced therapists there are clearly much more detailed discussions in greater depth elsewhere. If written for the advanced professional the book would be much longer, review more literature, and have many more references. But this effort is primarily designed for patients and for that group it is quite comprehensive.

I describe myself as psychoanalytically oriented and explain to my patients the difference between psychoanalysis and therapy guided by psychoanalytic principles. "Psychoanalytic" refers to an extensive field of study and practice, beginning with Sigmund Freud and grounded in ideas of internal and interpersonal conflict and unconscious mental processes. The therapy conducted by many therapists, while not labeled as psychoanalytic, rests on psychoanalytic principles, for example the concepts of transference and countertransference to be discussed later. Psychoanalytic therapy can be any number of sessions and duration can be as brief or as long as needed. Psychoanalysis, on the other hand, is more specialized, the most intensive and extensive form of therapy. It is not for the majority of people. It is frequent meetings(three to five sessions a week), typically continues for several years and must be conducted by a psychoanalyst. The training takes five or six years and sometimes longer. It is well worth keeping in mind that there are many individuals for whom psychoanalytic psychotherapy, with less frequent meetings is as effective or more so than psychoanalysis (Wallerstein,

1986). With experience therapists gradually come to believe in the usefulness of inquiry and exploration.

There are few professions both more taxing and rewarding than being a psychotherapist. It is our privilege as therapists that our courageous patients share the details of their hopes, fears, vulnerabilities, and most private thoughts and concerns. We are honored with the rich life stories entrusted to us. I often tell my patients of my appreciation for trust they extend to me.

In contrast to the view, held by some misguided and fearful people that therapy is for the weak, the use of therapy, in fact, requires strength. More courage is needed to tackle personal problems that to avoid them. In some ways, treatment is not easy. There are stresses on the patient and therapist. You must attend regularly, tolerate the financial sacrifice, make therapy a priority in your life. As patient you are faced with an ambiguous task with only a few guidelines to direct you. You will be invited to explore painful experiences involving fear, anger, shame, guilt and troubled relationships. Uncertainty, an inherent part of the therapy experience for both patients and therapists, is among the hardest feelings to tolerate. However, therapists are trained to deal with uncertainty. As you have not had such training, it is the therapist's job to educate as needed. If one is to err, it should be in the direction or more education rather then less. Our training and experience teach us that perseverance, for the most part, leads to understanding and reduction of symptoms but that experience and the confidence it generates has not been acquired by new patients.

There can be obvious rewards in learning about oneself, discovering previously unknown factors in our personalities and motivations, seeing ourselves and our relationships change as a result of new learning. Some have compared analytic therapy to peeling away layers or an archeological dig, making new discoveries with each successive layer, emphasizing the process of discovery. The connection with the therapist has the potential to become a unique source of attachment and security, a vehicle for self understanding, and is often more intimate than any other in one's life. No one is likely to get to know you as well. And that relationship can be particularly crucial in sustaining you during inevitable painful periods in the process.

In therapy, there are two people, each experiencing some of the tugs, pushes and pulls of close relationships. Therapist stresses are limited by the extent that the therapist attends to self-care, has a relatively satisfying life, and takes opportunities for ongoing supervision and education. The therapist may welcome his emotional reactions to the therapy as an indispensable source of information, not as much for the patient. The therapist expects that the patient's emotional involvement in therapy (as well as the therapist's emotional involvement) will open doors to important information and forecast major themes

I thank my patients who have played an indispensable role in my development as a person and clinician. My struggles with issues presented by my patients allow me to further explore my own internal landscape, for me a significant benefit of conducting psychotherapy. I think of many patients often and, it is primarily about and for them, that I write this book

I divide the book into five chapters. Chapter 1 reviews the reasons you might seek therapy and describes the frequently difficult task of finding a therapist. I offer a few suggestions to help. Chapter 2 describes concepts essential to understanding patients and psychotherapy. A goal even if not entirely possible is to demystify therapy. I explain the centrality of relationships in development, attachment, unconscious processes, defenses, boundaries, transference and countertransference. Involving oneself in therapy is a key to the resolution of relationship problems. In Chapter 3 I review symptoms of depression, anxiety and panic, and post traumatic stress. I attempt to demonstrate that symptoms have meaning. Chapter 4 reviews the stages of therapy and the potential gains. This section is an introduction to how the therapist thinks, why he behaves in certain ways and how he facilitates the therapy. To understand the therapy process means to grasp the concepts that guide the therapist's thinking. Along the way I provide illustrations of the interaction of therapist and patient. If you are better informed you can be a better partner to your therapist and a better therapist to yourself. Chapter 5 is to raise awareness of some half-hidden influences on therapy. I hope this knowledge will make therapy be more user friendly.

For clinical examples I use some material from therapies I conducted, some from the work of colleagues, some that were related to me in supervision and one who was a participant in research. I have made concerted efforts to disguise the identity of the patients who serve as examples. The way I work in therapy might meet with some degree of consensus among other therapists but my examples are neither the correct or best interventions. Therapy is more art than science and there are few if any correct answers, though some therapist comments are more useful than others. For economy of phrasing I will refer to patient and not client and therapist and not counselor. Also when referring to gender I will use "he" most of the time and "she" only when necessary to retain meaning.

Lastly gratitude to my readers. All three are supervising and training analysts and have supervised my therapy and psychoanalytic cases. Michael Harty, Ph.D. is a uniquely talented psychologist, a model of integrity, blessed with a poetic soul. Leonard Horwitz, Ph.D., a steadfast teacher, mentor and friend since 1965, past Director of Group Psychotherapy at Menninger and past president of The American Group Psychotherapy Association. Becquer Benalcazar, M.D., a friend for many years, a talented psychoanalyst, and current director of the Kansas City Psychoanalytic Institute.

Chapter 1

YOUR PSYCHOTHERAPY

A. Why Begin Psychotherapy

What is psychotherapy and why do people seek it? There are as many answers to that question as there are therapy patients. Needs for therapy stem from a broad range of problems: painful emotions including depression and high levels of anxiety, grief, and loss. Perhaps you are concerned as well with symptoms like inhibitions, phobias, sexual dysfunction, compulsions, addictions, irrational beliefs, to name some of the possibilities. In addition to the hope of reducing pain, you may hope to increase satisfaction, to live a more enlightened and aware life, to have better relationships, to find or create greater meaning in life, and are curious about how the mind works. Some patients begin therapy at the insistence of others, perhaps a boss or a spouse. For some initially reluctant fearful patients this kind of start may be necessary for them to begin the process. The patients initial complaints might be considered his symptoms, all of which have discernable meanings.

Therapy begins with two people meeting and interacting. The patient usually arrives with problems that cause pain and a vulnerable state of mind. The patient may know little or nothing about psychotherapy, perhaps his greatest familiarity from watching The Sopranos. In the beginning, the patient may be so distressed he will unquestionably, gratefully accept whatever efforts the therapist makes. The therapist has years of training in guidelines for proceeding, how to intervene, how to help lessen your discomfort. His first goal is to establish a safe atmosphere, and he will then gradually apply his knowledge to help reduce acutely painful states of mind, facilitate new learning and new perspectives. Hopefully, you will experience the therapist's wish to understand and help you. Gradually the typical initial idealization of the therapist will come closer to reality.

As you gradually feel a bit more secure, your therapist will get to know you by inviting you to discuss your thoughts, feelings, dreams, relationships, day to day challenges, and whatever is troubling you. He will help you learn that open, and frank discussion is most likely to lead to benefits. Your reasons for seeking help are unique and so there is no standard approach to the therapy. The therapist will try to find a close match between your needs and his contributions.

Soon you will discover that your initial concerns are in fact multifaceted and more complicated than thought at first blush. Let's take a patient from my practice as an example.

> He comes to therapy because of panic attacks that are increasingly frequent and severe. His general level of anxiety is increasing. I ask about his thoughts during and immediately preceding his episodes of panic. He is having frightening thoughts of harming certain people including his children. After we are both reassured that he would never intentionally hurt his children we can proceed with greater ease. Talking at length about his wife and children helps us discover that his wife has been frequently criticizing him to the children and undermines his parental authority. The patient keeps his eyes and mouth shut to this obviously dysfunctional parenting to avoid direct conflict with his wife. He unwittingly is directing his frustration toward the children. At this point, he is increasing awareness of his avoidance of conflict, how this problematic family pattern is playing out and affecting the children.
>
> During discussion of the patient's childhood, he recalled that his profoundly unhappy mother would look to him for comfort and criticize father at length for being inept and neglecting her. As a boy, the patient was the cozy confidant for his mother at the cost of

father's smoldering resentment, taking the form of a distant, critical attitude toward him. He was amazed to recognize the duplication of problems in his family of origin in his adult family. In childhood he learned fear and inhibition about being assertive or expressing anger. He feared alienating those he depended on (mother, wife, therapist). He came to recognize that his avoidant style of protecting relationships, his intimidation by the prospect of conflict, was costly in most areas of his life.

Many of this patient's initial concerns will be understood by the therapist as symptoms. So in this instance the symptom of panic attacks had several meanings one of which was his fear of acting on his anger and hurting others. Similarly, his inhibitions in self assertion contained a meaning of threatened abandonment and punishment.

Some patients arrive looking for quick, easy solutions because of a sense of urgency or desperation, fears of what might emerge over time. And occasionally the wish for a quick departure will result in premature endings.

> In the course of three meetings, a woman initially complained of a gradual loss of her once greater self-confidence. After some brief discussion she concluded that her therapy work was done. She came to realize that her confidence was severely affected when her husband had ongoing multiple affairs while, among other abuses, accusing her of not being as interested in sex as he thought she should. She had been devalued by the husband for many years. Though it may seem obvious to us that much more might have been usefully explored, in fact, she was satisfied with the realization that long years of being beaten down was the culprit. It was not that this situation was unconscious, but she was able to put the pieces together in a new way.
>
> Armed with this relatively new understanding she said that felt ready to demand more for herself. After two

sessions she announced that she would stop therapy. I told her that I hoped she would stay in therapy at least for a while longer as she had barely begun. She would not reconsider though I mentioned that we did not yet understand some important issues bringing her to therapy, namely why she put up with the marriage for so many years and why now she was leaving therapy before knowing what benefits awaited her. She left on a friendly note before I had a firm idea of why she was leaving, though I suspected that she was afraid that like her husband I would betray and abuse her and become critical. In retrospect I don't think that I gave enough weight to this woman preferring action over reflection, an issue which should have been attended to immediately.

Frequently as you think about your therapist's contributions to the dialogue those interventions will activate your introspective capacities and then curiosity about what follows (Allen, 2001).

B. Selecting a Therapist

Let's speculatively say that you have reached the point that you are suffering excessively. Perhaps you are defeating yourself and making the same mistakes over and over, having panic attacks and you want to get help. Or perhaps your supervisor at work has been taking notice of occasional angry outbursts, or a decline in work performance. Or your spouse urges you to get help with an addiction to porn, or alcohol, or drugs, or you suffer from an increasing number of physical problems for which no physical causes can be found. How do you find a well-qualified, skilled therapist who is a good match for you.

Some people will take an easy quick route and look in the phone book, a risky solution. There are so many different approaches or schools of therapy people looking for treatment may be understandably bewildered: transpersonal therapy, gestalt therapy, cognitive behavioral therapy, family systems therapy, existential therapy, based on meditation and imagery, Jungian therapy and others. Then there are different modalities of therapy: individual psychotherapy, group therapy, family or couple's therapy and in addition there are different types of counseling. Also there are therapies structured to deal with specific psychological conditions such as borderline personality disorder, addictions, eating disorders, trauma and phobias but for many people psychoanalytic therapy may be as effective or more so that the specialized modalities. One of the better known alternative therapies for trauma is called EMDR(Eye Movement Desensitization and Reprocessing). Once thought to be uniquely helpful for trauma this therapy has become a complicated form of therapy in itself.

Can I recommend one therapist or brand of therapy over another? Given that most therapies scientifically studied are shown to be useful I will speak for my fifty years in clinical practice, research and education. Rather than making specific suggestions I will provide some guidelines to aid in your selection. At the outset, I should state my bias. I am trained in psychotherapy based on psychoanalytic principles. For me that orientation is preferable because the training is typically extensive, rigorous, is imbedded in a long history of scholarship, and that's what I know. Also relatively longer term therapies, usually psychoanalytically oriented, have been shown to have longer lasting benefits (Shedler, 2010).

It is possible that a therapist will know of a specialized procedure that would benefit the patient, in which case a combination of treatments may be useful. I have found a combination of individual and group therapy to be effective with most of my patients. The individual therapy fuels use of the group and vice versa. I have extensive training in group dynamics and group therapy, which no doubt shapes my therapy preferences. Other therapists perhaps depending on their training specialties will have their own preferences for combinations of treatments.

Often therapy is usefully supplemented by medication. It is common knowledge among psychotherapists that the combination of therapy and medication in the majority of instances is more effective than either alone. Other treatments I have often found to be useful additions to individual therapy are, couples or family therapy and guided meditation.

Occasionally different medications may be combined as in bipolar disorders in which an antidepressant and a mood stabilizer may both be prescribed. You might consider family or couples therapy, or therapy for a child of the patient when the marriage or the children become an ongoing preoccupation in the therapy that significantly distracts from the patient's adequate attention to himself.

Psychoanalytically oriented therapy and psychoanalysis

I am trained as a psychoanalyst. That extensive training experience adds immeasurably to my therapy skills. Most psychoanalytic therapists have not been trained as analysts, nor is that necessary. Rather many therapists study analytic therapy in programs designated for that purpose, usually at a post doctoral level. I designed and administered one such program under the auspices of the Kansas City Psychoanalytic Institute. I find that it is also helpful that I have some training in group therapy, couple's therapy, biofeedback and relaxation techniques. Some patients are helped by being seen simultaneously in individual therapy, group therapy, couple's therapy and having a psychiatrist prescribe medication. If you have doubts about the extent of the therapist's clinical experience or training do not hesitate to ask. As you would assess many people from whom you are buying a service you will want to evaluate the therapists services and practice.

It may help to distinguish between training in psychoanalytic therapy and psychoanalysis. Psychoanalytic training beyond a graduate degree typically involves several years of seminars, having one's own analysis as a patient and conducting analysis with several patients with intensive supervision. That training takes 5 to 6 years plus. Psychiatrists, social workers, psychologists and a few other specialties can obtain either postgraduate psychotherapy training or training to become a psychoanalyst. The training in analytic psychotherapy is usually two years in duration with academic courses, group discussion of therapy cases, supervision and hopefully having psychotherapy as a patient. It is my opinion, shared by many other therapists, that it is a serious omission to learn therapy without having the experience of being a patient.

Too often therapists are selected analogous to spinning a roulette wheel, selecting from an insurance company's list of 'providers' or from other directories, perhaps just listing their degree. In my opinion, one's particular graduate degree may have little bearing on that person's skills as a therapist. A major disadvantage of selecting from insurance company rosters is that many of the most experienced therapists are not listed. It is somewhat better to have a referral from someone who knows and trusts the therapist. Though I know the majority of you may not know such a person.

Admittedly finances are a factor in the therapist you select or is selected for you. Low income people are likely to have a therapist from a community mental health center. Many have insurance provided by a business. Patients with the most financial resources will have the greatest choice of therapists. For those without commercial insurance there may be help through the social welfare system.

I will mention a few guidelines that may help you select a therapist. The therapist should be well trained. Most patients do not ask about the therapist's credentials. However, it is OK and perhaps even wise for you to ask about the therapist's credentials. You should feel sufficiently comfortable that you can freely ask questions and relatively confident that you can be personally compatible. For example, if the therapist is a strong public advocate for certain values or causes, as a patient I might not be able to work with him. This is a highly individual matter involving personal sensitivities.

Some other red flags might be the therapist seeming to be too concerned about a particular subject such as money or sex, showing indications of inattentiveness, having an overly intimate style. I had a colleague who was a bit to eager to initiate hugs and to share personal details of his private life. It will take a few sessions together to make an initial assessment of these issues. Take your time! It may be helpful to listen carefully to the therapist's contributions to a discussion of goals you want to accomplish. Is he quite interested, seem distracted, bored, overly excited, all reactions worth asking about.

For some patients, the gender of their therapist seems quite important. So you might want to think about whether you will be more comfortable with a male or female therapist. If you have strong feelings about it be sure to share that preference. If there is not a gender choice give therapy a try with the therapist of the non-preferred gender and discuss with the therapist how that is working for you. Arguably more important than gender is the extent of the therapists training and experience.

One of the less widely known sources for psychotherapy or psychoanalysis is in psychoanalytic institutes. It is relatively unknown that Institutes may offer a referral service and often are prepared to offer quite low cost analysis with students of psychoanalysis who require cases for their training.

Some people not familiar with psychotherapy may expect a traditional doctor-patient relationship with the treater as as ultimate authority and the patient as a relatively passive recipient. In this instance you might assume that you can sit back, relax, and enjoy the benefits which will flow to you. You will be more a partner with much of the work relying on your effort, initiative and creativity. Your therapist will act more like a guide than a director. Once you experience that your therapist can help relieve your distress and pain you may begin to look forward to your sessions.

Chapter 2

ESSENTIAL CONCEPTS

A. We are a product of our relationships

Much about therapy will make greater sense to you if you know that it is at core an interpersonal, relationship process. This chapter is intended to show some of the many ways we are imbedded in and influenced by relationships, all of our lives. It follows that most psychological problems find expression in faulty relationships, an inability to form and sustain relationships. An essential fact to know about people is that their psychological makeup, strengths, and vulnerabilities, are rooted in relationships, those in infancy, childhood, and adulthood.
It is no more that a few hours after birth that an infant looks for a human face. It is as though we are hard wired, genetically predisposed, to relate to others from the beginning (Beebe & Lachman, 2002). Then if on balance care givers help the child to be comforted a relationship will be constructed and the child will be placed on a road to increasing capacity for self reliance. However, if those basic needs for contact, safety and comfort are thwarted because we suffer severe neglect or abuse, there will be consequences for development of our mental life, even for our survival. Because of these considerations I strive for therapy to be shaped not by technique or other mechanical considerations but by a human interactional process.

A brief example: a patient sees my position about the fee as set by institutional standards. I clarified that whatever external standards were involved we set the fee in accord with what we agree is fair and consistent with our discussion of the matter. In this way, we make external influences less important determinants than our relationship.

Each time the therapist offers you an opportunity to negotiate he is emphasizing that therapy is essentially an interactional human exchange.

Children and caretakers

Although I will describe some parents as complicit in their child's disturbance, my intent is not to assign blame. Nor is blaming justified. Children respond in remarkably different and creative ways to what they are given. There is no simple cause and effect. The family does, undeniably, exert an influence. But the distinction between causation and influence is important to understand people. Perhaps parental influence is most evident in their child's attitudes and expectations, those aspects of parenting in which the child is immersed. Some people dislike a language of relativity rather than cause and effect because the former increases complexity. There can be little subtlety or basis for nuanced discussion if problems are reduced to polarities of good vs. bad or right vs. wrong. The study of psychotherapy yields neither facts or answers but rather focuses on engaging in a meaningful growth promoting relationship and dialogue. There is a definite trend for psychological problems to be transmitted across several generations.

Moment by moment, loops of mutual influence and exchange accrue between the child and others, gradually forming relationship patterns. These patterns become habitual, or as we might say, "internalized.

> For example, the child smiles and reaches for contact. If the parent is too preoccupied, depressed, or unavailable, and if this pattern of non-responding persists the child, having made multiple failed efforts, will eventually give up, becoming depressed, lethargic and withdrawn. If the neglect continues for prolonged periods of time, the child won't come to confidently know what it means to be human, to respond and be responded to.

> Another example of the early role of relationships on development might be the child, who slightly older, shows initiative in a variety of ways. If those efforts are not recognized and rewarded, the child will not

see any connection between his effort and resulting changes. Then, the capacity to initiate may become quite conflicted or impaired.

Imagine for example the child's first smile, first steps, first words passing without recognition or celebration. It is not difficult to understand how these parent-child relationships gone awry can become the groundwork for psychological problems in adulthood.

Parents threatened by their children

Some troubled parents are threatened by their child's development.

I recall from my own practice a woman bitterly telling me about how as an adolescent when she dressed her best for a first prom her father, unsure of his sexuality and threatened by his daughter's sexuality responded "go upstairs and take off that makeup young lady. You look like a tramp."

It took years in therapy for this woman to fully realize the damage done to her self esteem by a pattern of insensitive and cruel behavior in her family. She was an angry woman who had every right to be angry as she lacked parental affirmation, parents who would respond with pleasure and pride with each of their daughters steps forward. It is fairly common when a patient works on relations with parents that there are subsequent improvements in relations with their children.

Neglectful parents

A young man in my practice, described that his parents never came to events in which he was involved or performed; football, debate, a school play. He gradually learned that, for his parents he seemed to barely exist, that his excelling in anything was unwelcome. Anything that would naturally call for a parent's recognition failed to elicit a response. Later in life he struggled mightily to advance himself professionally, accompanied by a "what's the use" inertia. He performed tasks because he must, not because of gratification in doing so. Any task he tackled was accompanied by a feeling that it was pointless, useless, empty, meaningless. His parents were so removed from their son because of their unfortunate circumstances with their parents. His father never learned affection for children and his mother was too emotionally distant to notice any problems. It is difficult to imagine that the patient could have formed secure attachments.

Self Absorbed Parents

There are self-preoccupied parents who view their children as extensions of themselves.

The children are expected to reflect back to the parents an image that the parent's need to see. So the child's successes will be treated primarily as placing the parents in a good light, perhaps as perfect parents, rather than due to the credit of the youngster. Even failures are not acknowledged because they do not reinforce the parents preferred self-image. Later, as an adult, the patient thought that he could not produce anything of merit. This youngster's efforts were not recognized and in that sense he felt that he did not exist.

Chaotic parents

Even in the most severe disturbances, like schizophrenia, we know that relationships are crucial, that the family relationships and atmosphere should be calm, not overstimulating. Caregivers who overexcite, excessively blame, and react to the infant in unpredictable or bizarre ways lead to the child being unable to form a survival strategy or sense of safety (Lichtenberg, 2005).

Our selection bias

As we mature, we may select a spouse, friend or significant other who is similar to our parents in positive and negative ways. We seem to be more comfortable with the familiar no matter how dysfunctional that may be. Some people go to great lengths to chose someone who seems the opposite of their parents.

From my current life, as I entered my senior years and aging became a major issue I hoped to recognize that I do not have to age in ways similar to my parents and grandparents. My prior analysis is helping me achieve that goal. I do see remarkable parallels between my father and myself. The issue is not that I will be like parents in ways but whether I can retain similarities that do well for me and dispel or modify those that do not. This differentiated response to parents is beneficial in any circumstance often aided by therapy. I sometimes tell a patient that whether you are like your parents or not like your parents you miss the point and loose your basic reference to yourself. In your years when your parents are elderly caretaking roles are reversed with the possibility of replaying your child-adult scenarios with them. Sometimes as parents become elderly and roles reverse there are new possibilities for repair of that damaged relationship.

> One patient had a stormy relationship with her father. As he grew older he became increasingly dependent on her for caretaking, difficult for him because he did not rely on anyone and distrusted those he might depend on. He was a difficult man who had been quite unkind to his children and had lived in marginally ethical ways. When near the end of his days he had no choice but to turn more and more to his daughter and found that he could count on her he was surprised that she was kind and loving to him. By the time of his death they were able to express love for one another.

My hope is that I have provided enough information to underscore that we are all embedded in relationships life-long. As relationships are so influential from the start, they should also help to correct problematic internal states. Making such corrections is where psychotherapy may enter the picture. Therapy can be a corrective emotional experience. It holds and contains us without criticism or judgment and helps us to understand how certain relationships have gone awry. Relatively long-term therapy may produce long-lasting change, even affecting brain functioning (Cozolino, 2002).

Clinician researchers are now examining the effect of coaching in parental skills for underprivileged mothers and their infants, with resulting benefits to the child. They focus on helping the mothers read and understand their infant's emotional states. This kind of parental instruction would likely benefit most, if not all, parents. It is a wonder that so many of us turn out relatively OK considering that the most important job in our lives, parenting, we have little training or guidance and stumble along on our own.

B. Attachment Is a Path To Our Styles of Relating

This section is an elaboration of the prior one on the centrality of relationships in forming the mind. This part of the book together with the last is intended to help you appreciate the crucial role of detailed exploration of your relationships. The attachment issues we will discuss form the basic building blocks of the child's mental processes. They refer to aspects of the mind which are mostly not conscious. These qualities play particularly significant roles in the formation of moods, attitudes, various tolerances and vulnerabilities. Were your mother or father depressed in your infancy, or inaccessible for other reasons? If so was adequate substitute mothering provided? Was your family in a state of turmoil during your infancy and if so what might the effect have been on earliest attachments and security. All of the factors above will each have their influence. As an example of extremely disturbed surroundings, Anna Freud studied the damage done to children during wartime London by separation and relocation. Others have studied the special effects on children of parents who suffered the Holocaust. These children suffer more than the expectable degree of guilt and seemed to carry some of the parents angst with them.

Family emotional atmosphere and fit

As I imply, crucial parental influence is not limited to specific parental behavior but also includes the predominant emotional atmosphere in the family including the fit of the child with the mother. What about the cultural influences of the day? One can hear those factors in the verbal play between mother and infant and listening to fairy tales, which frequently portray current cultural values. Some secure mothers and babies seem to mold naturally to each other while other pairings seem awkward, not having a mutual fit. The mother may be so uncomfortable and the child so non-receptive that instead of mutual fitting and molding to one another, mother appears to be holding a bundle of sticks. Perhaps in a therapy that lasts for years some of these developmentally early issues will arise as partial influences of moods.

Styles of attachment

Concepts emerging from the extensive study of attachment between child and mother have become important in most therapist's views of patient's traits and behavior. Such concepts provide models for types of relationships as well as types of therapist-patient interaction. These ideas refer to styles of attachment formed in early childhood and continuing throughout our lifetime. The researchers observed separation and reunion with mother and described the child's styles of response: the "secure", the avoidant, the resistant and "disorganized," each stemming from a particular kind of relationship with the mother(Ainsworth et al, 1978; Target, 2002).

Securely attached children are upset when the mother leaves and happy when she returns, the response we might expect. They are very aware of mother leaving and seek nearness to her when she returns. Security is quickly reestablished. Crucially important is that the mothers in this category are sensitively attuned to their infant, and respond to the baby's signals rather than imposing their own needs on the infant. Secure attachment is among the best protections against trauma and distress of various kinds. And attachment is necessary for the regulation of distress and helps build mental capacities that the person can bring to subsequent interactions (Fonagy et al 2002).

The avoidant insecurely attached children are disturbed by separation, and when mother returns, they seek to be close but are resentful, angry and may be hard to soothe. So a conflictual emotional situation develops of wanting closeness to the mother but resenting her. You may hear an emotional push-pull which may be difficult for mother and child. The anxious resistant child is preoccupied with attachment and not easily comforted when mother returns. These mothers may not be attuned to their infant's needs and respond reluctantly without providing sufficient interaction. Observing this pair one can sense their disengagement.

The next category of disorganized attachment is marked by the lack of any organized pattern. The child's behavior and emotion seem fragmented and hard to read. The disorganized style tends to be associated with severe disturbances and severe forms of mistreatment including various forms of abuse and neglect. These infants may suddenly turn away from mother or manifest episodes of aggression. Even when frightened the infant will not seek out mother. There is no safe haven. These infants may alternate between isolation and desperate clinging. These forms of attachment will last a lifetime. For example, the securely attached child will be inclined to develop trusting relationships with security prominent in a wide range of attachments. These forms of attachment will also depend on the behavior of the child's caretakers. The style of attachment will eventually become part of the response to groups and institutions.

Perhaps in reading about these patterns of separation and attachment you can place yourself, as a child, and as an adult, in one of these categories more that another or shifting from one style to another. These attachment patterns, while tending to persist into adulthood, have been complicated and changed by your adult years. The last three categories involve pain for the child and the caretaker. Aspects of therapy may exert a corrective influence. For the insecurely attached child, the consistency, reliability, emotional presence, and responsiveness of the therapist set the right(holding) atmosphere to correct for early parental inconsistencies.

You might think about your emotional style of dealing with separation and reunion. Are you sometimes surprised by the intensity of reaction to your therapist's absences, and if so does this represent a tendency in relationships outside therapy? Perhaps anger toward a boyfriend who is often late goes a little over the top. The closeness that seems to cling and suffocate may relate to insecure attachment. As would cutting off emotionally from your spouse when she returns from a visit with her parents. Do you seem to constantly carry a sense of insecurity with you? Any of these responses, in-so-far as they create problems in your relationships, may point in the direction of an attachment style that causes pain that you may wish to explore and change. The parents of children in this "insecure" category may be unresponsive to the needs of the child for warmth and comfort. These mothers may be detached and unresponsive, interacting in a mechanical ways with the infant, taking little pleasure in that interaction.

A lack of attachment

I'll close with a slightly different perspective coming from an insightful classic American film. An alone and dying Charles Foster Kane holds a crystal ball containing an image of winter. His grip loosens, and the ball falls to the floor, shattering into a thousand pieces, like the fragmented pieces of his life. He utters two words, perhaps his last," Rose Bud". Kane's tragedy is that though one of the world's richest men, he has alienated those who cared for him. He could not allow them to become important to him. At the last moment of his life, he cries out for his only meaningful childhood attachment, his sled "Rosebud." In this poignant, sad scene Orson Wells proclaims: How crucial human attachments are for one's life, in infancy and later and how empty we are without them. I have known a few people like Kane, who, without intensive, long-term psychotherapy, specifically psychoanalysis, would have ended up much like him. There are many examples in classical literature of people who suffer from a profound emptiness echoing the same theme, Dicken's Scrouge, Keat's Ozymandias, Melville's Billy Bud, Shakespeare's Richard the third, Wells' film Citizen Kane, Poe's Dorian Gray, the film Alfie and more recently Night Crawler.

C. Unconscious processes: Feelings and Thoughts Which We reject

The history of the idea of unconscious mental processes is long and complicated. Freud is the best-known proponent of the idea as an aid to understanding mental life. The working of unconscious processes will play a major role in your psychotherapy and in your life. I will try to illustrate the importance of our unconscious mental processes.

One meaning of the unconscious is for mental contents close to conscious awareness and may quickly become conscious as one turns attention to them. So I may not be thinking of the movie I saw last week but a mere reference to the film will bring it to mind along with associations. Sometimes this is referred to as preconscious memory.

Unconscious guilt: I am not worthy

More relevant to this discussion there is another kind of unconscious in which ideas are dismissed from consciousness because to keep them in mind is painful, causes anxiety, shame, and anticipated disapproval.

> One fellow told me that years ago he briefly experienced intense and uncomfortable sexual desire for his sister accompanied by vivid visual imagery. For this anxious "uptight" fellow, the licentious thoughts were more than he could tolerate. This impulse was sufficiently disturbing that he drove it from his mind, and it remained inaccessible until recalled in therapy. In later, years he had a secretary who unconsciously reminded him of that sister. He provoked arguments with her to ensure a safe sense of distance from the forbidden. He had no conscious awareness of the reason for alienating the secretary until explored in the therapy. It helps to understand this man to know that he was raised in an ultra-religious family. The mere mention of the word sex was forbidden.

The historically difficult concept of unconscious guilt is a puzzle to people because of the difficulty of grasping how one can feel guilty without knowing the particular thoughts or actions about which one is feeling guilty. Not so complicated when using clinical examples.

> A child has been taught that he is not "good", of value, because in early years that lesson was communicated to him by unhappy parents, with an implication that he was "bad". They blamed him for causing their unhappiness. Later that person without thinking of himself as bad, acts in self-defeating ways, allowing himself little in the way of success or gratification. The person seems to spoil opportunities to feel better or for potential success. Exploration may expose the feeling of badness, first imbued by parents and taken-in by the patient, as the unconscious source of self-defeating behavior. This guilt dynamic is common in those who question their value or worth leading to profound disturbances in self-esteem. Therapy can help make that childhood belief conscious and, therefore, available for correction.

Dreams and the unconscious

One aspect of therapy that can dramatically demonstrate workings of unconscious processes is work on dreams. That work often results in the patients first awareness of the existence and importance of thoughts, feelings and assumptions over which he has little awareness or control. In contrast to some writings on dream symbols, understanding the meanings in the dream requires discussion and exploration of the dreamer's associations to the dream. There is no easy link between symbols and what they symbolize. In fact, a single part of the dream may represent different meanings in different contexts. Consequently, therapists will ask for the patient's thoughts (associations) about various parts of the dream.

Let's consider the appearance of a house in a dream. For some people houses they have lived in represent images of themselves, their relationships or a particular situation from either the past or present. A revealing exercise is to ask the client to draw a house and then collect their thoughts about the details of the drawing. I have found that a ground level often relates to issues of being grounded, or not, stability or instability. Sometimes one's aspirations relate to themes about the higher stories. The basement is often a metaphor well suited to represent our unconscious mental processes, that which is below the surface, of which we are unaware. A few examples follow.

The dreams of one person who suffered from life-long periodic depressions had the repeated theme of cracks appearing in the ceilings and walls of his home. When repaired the "flaws" soon reappeared, generating feelings of desperate futility and failure of his efforts to repair the damage. The theme of feeling flawed as a person and repeating the same failed efforts over and over closely paralleled his self-image. His dreams contained the same terror of the basement that he experienced in his childhood home. From his various other thoughts about the dream I came to realize, along with the patient, that his distant hypercritical father and a seductive depriving mother symbolically resided in a dark corner of the basement behind the furnace. This area seemed to him to be particularly secluded and menacing. Importantly the patient vaguely recalled mother responding to his childhood misbehavior by threatening to put him in the furnace. He could clearly remember her threat but had no memory of the terror he must have felt. Later dreams revealed that the cracks were due to a vacuous space undermining the structure. The patient was thereby, unconsciously suggesting that his security was weakened by an early deficit, deprivation and a consequent sense of emptiness.

When confronted with new challenges, this bright and resourceful man's first reaction was always to feel deskilled, lost, bereft of the nurture and stable structure needed to move forward. Gradually learning about previously unconscious events leading to his poor self-esteem and weak self-confidence he could face and more realistically evaluate his self-doubts. A phrase that arose was to purge "the ghosts in the attic". He also discovered that seeking help, as in the therapy, could be strengthening rather than undermining.

For another patient dreams of cracks in the wall of his home, which could not be repaired, but at best camouflaged, were linked to, at least one serious head injury. These "cracks in the head" were in all probability a source of his moderate attention deficit disorder. Though he knew in a cloudy way that something about his mental functioning was not normal he had little consciously formulated sense of ADD until in his 40s when conflicts with his wife revealed the problem. His ADD caused problems in memory that were interpreted by his wife as evidence of how little he cared about her. After all, she thought if he cared he would remember birthdays, anniversaries, holidays and all five items she asked asked him to get at the grocery store. He would usually remember three. Neither of them had any idea that the patient's errors and forgetting had little to do with caring and were more connected to the husband's deficits. Because the struggles between the couple about these issues continued for years, there was a lot of resentment to sort out. The couple's relationship improved with sessions to educate them about ADD and provide a forum for dealing with their accumulated resentments.

D. Defenses: Our means of Reducing Emotional Pain

I have chosen psychological defense as a frame of reference which may in part illustrate how the mind works. Over our lifetimes, more so in childhood, we develop methods for protecting ourselves against emotional pain, mostly anxiety and depression. Defenses, repeated and elaborated over time, have often been supported by parents, and become our habitual means of dealing with psychological discomfort. Each type of defense plays a part in the way we think and in our relationships.

I wish to underscore that the defenses are essentially interpersonal in their construction.

Repression as censorship

We may respond to painful, forbidden thoughts and memories by banishing them from our mind (repression), a process which takes place mostly unconsciously, that is we are unaware of banishing the threatening ideas and feelings. Because anxiety laden thoughts may always find ways into consciousness in disguised forms, the defense of repression, to be effective, must exclude an increasingly extensive array of associated thoughts, feelings and memories. The results are that major areas of experience may seem a void, marked by absence. The person who relies on repression may seem naive and unknowing due to the exclusion from consciousness of the experiences and knowledge which are not permissible. Repressive tendencies generalize to thought style as in a tendency to be closed to ideas, turn away from learning or from intellectual curiosity.

Dissociation as a division or breaking-up of experience

We may also expel thoughts and feelings experienced as dangerous in a manner referred to as dissociation. This defense is often a consequence of abuse, particularly sexual abuse but it is evident in most traumatized people. Dissociation more than repression operates in an all or none fashion. Trauma might be considered an experience which overwhelms ones cognitive and emotional capacities. When traumatized we may retain a visual memory of the trauma but split off (dissociate) the emotions associated with that trauma. For example, one may have a repeated visual image of the trauma entirely void of the emotions involved. Or similarly emotions associated with trauma may arise though completely divorced from any memory of the trauma, as in panic attacks.

In effect, with dissociation we split the trauma onto more manageable pieces and thereby reduce the destabilizing and overwhelming impact of all aspects (emotions, thoughts, memory) occurring simultaneously.

Similarly, people will often report that they view the traumatic event from an uninvolved distance, as in dispassionately watching a movie.

Denial and avoidance as negation and flight

As pain occurs we automatically rely on defenses which over time, become habitual means of dealing with psychological discomfort. Defenses simultaneously protect from pain and cause other troubles. So the use of repression may result in a chronic alertness to danger (tension), and/ or an unpleasant sense of emptiness. Each defense will play a part in the way we think, our thought style and in our relationships. So the person who relies heavily on repression may be quite naive in some ways due to the knowledge which is not allowable. The defense of denial works by simply denying that a disturbing event, thought, emotion, is occurring, a sticking one's head in the sand approach, with the disadvantages to the individual of relying on stupidity.

A defensive stance related to the defense described here is called avoidance, and is just as the word implies, anything conflictual is simply avoided. Then one is often blindsided, as in repeatedly making the same mistake, because of depriving oneself of crucial life information. We likely all know of people who repeat the same errors as though unable to learn form experience. The manner in which a person comes to prefer one defense over another is complicated but depends on genetic predisposition together with specific early childhood experiences including the parents unwittingly conveying their own preferred defenses. You may know families which turn the other way, don't look, don't see, don't explore, where it is clear that avoidance and denial prevail.

Reaction formation as purging and transformation.

A defense that may bewilder others is called reaction formation, a turning of anger or aggression into its opposite. The patient has unconsciously tried to purge their personality of anger. About this person a friend might say: "He is so sweet and nice. When someone steps on his toes or says something offensive he becomes even sweeter. It can be annoying. Do you notice how often he hurts himself, breaks an arm, stubs a toe, sprains a rist". The friend is on the verge of recognizing where the patient's anger goes, toward himself. You may have observed that some people in this category may be susceptible to eating disorders.

You have likely heard of a defense called "projection". This is simply to attribute one's unacceptable thoughts or feelings to another thereby feeling rid of those qualities in oneself. This tendency may serve to reduce discomfort about oneself. On the down-side extremes of projection lead to suspiciousness or outright paranoia. A painful sense of emptiness follows from expulsion of significant parts of the self onto the outside world.

Obsessive compulsive traits aim to eliminate disturbing emotion.

A defensive style with which most of us are familiar is referred to as obsessive-compulsive. Here the emotion is squeezed out of situations in preference for reason, logic, and order. Compulsive people may not understand emotions in themselves or others. Empathy is difficult for them to achieve because they are without recognition of emotion in day to day life, and as a determiner of behavior. They may be experienced as tedious, humorless, nit-picking. They get lost in the trees and don't recognize the forest. Of course these traits vary widely across different obsessive compulsive people. The more obsessionally inclined are known to take hold of certain ideas and not let them go. The link between obsessionalism and guilt is sometimes obvious. Consider for example Shakespeare's Lady MacBeth who ritually and incessantly washed her hands to symbolically rid herself of the guilt of having murdered the king.

Projective identification as expulsion and control

The last defense I will discuss, related to projection, perhaps the most complicated, is referred to as projective identification. This defense more than any other is interpersonal in nature, in that it requires two people in interaction. An example: a person who tends to feel guilty about his angry feelings may be ripe for the person who wishes to rid themselves of their anger and suggests to the guilty person that he is the angry one. A person wishes to expel and control certain feelings that trouble him, finds a receptive place in the other and, partly through suggestion, pushes their unwelcome feelings into the other. The recipient may feel coerced into feeling something they don't ordinarily feel, or simply feel disturbed, suddenly feeling "not me". The person using projective identification then sees their unwelcome thought or feeling in the other, as containing their unwanted emotion and tries to manipulate the other while unaware of the feeling in themselves. The defense is often successful in that the other is actually induced to experience the projected thoughts or feelings. To further complicate the matter the defense operates unconsciously. Some experts in child development have described projective identification as one of the earliest forms of communication between child and caretaker in which currents of feeling run back and forth between the two, a form of mutual sending and receiving of emotional messages.

Now, having described how the defenses work, you might ask what is the relevance of that knowledge to being a patient in psychotherapy. It may help add a bit to understand how your mind works, it says something of the picture you unconsciously convey to your therapist and may help to understand why you react in therapy and in your life the ways you do. As a potentially instructive exercise you might think about where you see yourself in the array of defensive styles and how that style effects your self image and relationships

E. Boundaries: Where do I end and you begin?

Boundaries protect and confine

Some aspects of therapy will be new to patients including therapist behavior that stems from his sensitivity to boundaries or limits, a universal part of training to be a psychotherapist. Diverse guidelines are intended to provide regulation of certain aspects of patient-therapist interaction. The guidelines, often in the form of statements of ethical standards by national or state professional organizations, specify what interactions fall in or outside ethical and legal limits. An example is the sanctions against patient and therapist sexual engagement. Other guidelines may focus on therapist exploitation of the therapy relationship Typically there are no official guidelines for common courtesy and kindness. How we define these boundaries and in particular how we negotiate them can be crucial in making the treatment as useful as possible. One of the essential boundaries is defined by standards of confidentiality. We don't get the best start in being required to report ordinarily confidential information to insurance companies.

The rude therapist

Therapy is neither friendship or primarily counseling or advice. Consequently, aspects of the therapist's behavior or interventions may be mystifying to the patient. For example, the patient may not understand the therapists not giving lots of advice or not accepting an invitation to meet for coffee or hesitating to answer a personal question. I knew a therapist who, unfortunately, often took phone calls during appointments, generating a quiet resentment in the client. In part because the patient was unaware this rude behavior violated not only common courtesy but as well a therapy boundary, he was reluctant to take this problem up with the therapist.

Boundaries are most clear when they are violated

For the therapy to be a safe, trustworthy situation, certain boundaries or limits will be maintained. Confidentiality and its exceptions are one of those limits. Rarely the usual limits are grossly violated, sexually, or in some other inappropriate ways, with disastrous consequences.

> I saw a professional in therapy who became sexually involved with one of his patients. Betraying a sense of omnipotence, he thought that his love would save this young woman from being the lost, very ill waif she was. In some ways the woman represented a part of himself. He seemed a lost person with a desperate depressive hunger for attachment. Expectably he also harbored a deep seated resentment of authority. His childhood circumstances established expectations of extreme closeness to mother and father's resentment of him. He was replaying the earlier family situation in therapy with the therapist in the role of father whom

he both feared and defied. I informed him on several occasions that although some of his intentions were understandable the result could be that he would destroy the therapy with his patient, thereby harm the patient and possibly end his career He had already been reported to appropriate ethics and licensing boards. His collaboration was strained, at best grudging. I was faced with whether to end his therapy. To this day I am not sure whether there was a best or better solution to my quandary. He was fired from his job, quit therapy and left town.

Fifteen years or so later I was surprised by a letter from him. He said that my not having abandoned him and not having wavered from my stand that his behavior was self destructive and destructive to his patient, had later saved his career and he profusely expressed his gratitude. He rescued me from the sense that his therapy was a total failure. I can not account for his seeming turnaround. I don't know what happened to his patient. However seldom is there a good outcome to such instances because the therapist and his patient spoil her therapy, with one result being an enhancement of a sense in both people of their power to destroy. Worse yet in the name of love.

You may occasionally hear of questionable therapist behavior. It is important that whatever question may be raised in you by such reports be discussed with your therapist. Otherwise your doubts may become an undermining stream below the surface.

A variety of more benign boundary issues will arise for you and your therapist to deal with. How will your therapist respond to a gift, an invitation to a social occasion, a graduation or a wedding? Perhaps, if the therapist will not attend, a compromise is possible. At the least it is reasonable for you to expect an explanation of the reasons for the refusal. I think that you should always express your wishes and then you and your therapist work with it, often with the result being an improved relationship, an improved alliance. Such negotiation stands in marked contrast to rigid and authoritarian therapist behavior that may drive important relationship issues underground.

Another boundary issue recently and increasingly occupying discussion is therapist self-disclosure. Therapists debate when, what, and where for the therapist to disclose personal feelings with the patient. I think, though not sure, that most therapists feel comfortable disclosing fondness, and admiration for the patient. Disclosure of negative feelings is more complicated. An example might be "You are such a decent and likeable guy but the contempt you show for others is offensive." The practice of therapist self disclosure is another area where boundaries have become more flexible over the years and which underscore that so many are permeable and subject to change. What might be the pros and cons of the therapist disclosing personal information about himself to the patient? The usefulness of disclosure may depend on the stage of the therapy, the patient's sensitivities, the therapist's good judgment and the genuineness of that sharing of information. Certainly the therapist should not share his personal information indiscriminently and yet it is important for him to express himself with some degree of spontenaity. Otherwise he risks the process being stilted and too formal.

Also to be taken into account when you and your therapist are in a social situation, perhaps an accident, is how to handle introductions. You may not be comfortable introducing him as "my therapist". It may be awkward as well for the therapist, who does not want to inadvertently violate confidentiality by revealing that you are his patient. In extended therapy the two might take an opportunity to discuss such possibilities and reach an agreement about how to proceed. If I happen to see the patient outside of therapy I usually look for clues from him and do not take initiative except perhaps for a friendly handshake. It is the process of patient and therapist working to produce compromises that is useful to the patient and to the process of therapy.

Negotiation of boundaries provide opportunities for growth.

A manipulative, very troubled patient insisted I hold her hand to help reduce her anxiety and provide the comforting she needed. We discussed this and its implications. I acknowledged we were getting close to the limits of my comfort and we reached a compromise that she would hold a finger when she thought that was needed. Perhaps the compromise was not crucial but what it symbolized and the process of together working through a solution was crucial. After these events the patient was noticeably less provocative, defiant and hostile. From that point on emphasis was on how intensely the patient felt attached to me.

One patient brought me a bagel every appointment for years. We would talk and joke about it. I expressed my appreciation for her gift and her kindness while keeping some focus on the meaning of the gift, namely her wish to nurture me to assure I would do the same for her and eventually such gifts seemed to diminish in emotional significance. If compromises are presented in your therapy both you and your therapist will want to take into account which decisions will preserve and perhaps enhance the usefulness of the therapy and is fair for both parties. Getting to that point will be helpful to you.

A slippery slope

Attending a special event at a patient's request may occupy a significant amount of the therapist's time. Usually, two reasonable people can work this out but it is still an area of sensitivity for patients. The outcome is less important than the dialogue. Occasionally I would send a client a postcard when on vacation or bring a small gift for the patient from an extended trip. For some patients, the proof that out of sight is not out of mind may help the relationship. Similarly, when on a business trip to Japan I brought my psychoanalyst a small but meaningful gift. Personal engagement with a subject often drives an artist to paint or a photographer to photograph, and so it is with psychotherapy. That engagement is mandatory for effective psychotherapy. Some therapists and some patients may be hesitant to let their involvement show.

There are many references in the psychotherapy literature to a "slippery slope", the idea that a hug, for example, might drift in the direction of grossly inappropriate(sexual) behavior.

In a prolonged therapy my attractive female patient made overt detailed sexual proposals. I informed her that I was flattered but a bit inhibited and consequently uncomfortable with these overtures. I wished to avoid any criticism of her and once again underscore our interaction. The issue was only partly about sex but also about power and was to test whether the relationship was worthy of trust or was as corruptible as so many of her other relationships. Her proposals were less a slope than a cliff.

The "slope" depends entirely on the particular therapist, his degree of depressive vulnerability and neediness or, much worse, a predatory streak. If a therapist feels that in the context of considerable intimacy he can not keep reasonable limits, he should resume his personal treatment, exit the field or both. The idea of a slippery slope into inappropriate behavior can promote caution and can also frighten and inhibit new therapists and secondarily create anxiety in the patient.

One might generalize and say that boundaries should be sufficient to ensure the safe continuation of therapy and not so tight as to inflict unnecessary injury, stifle or inhibit. Many of the boundaries relevant to you and your therapist will be like those you encounter in your life. A message that I hope you will take away from this discussion is the idea that boundary issues should be amenable to discussion and negotiation in such a way as to facilitate the therapy.

F. Transference and Countertransference

Transference shows in emotionally colored perceptions of the therapist

I view transference and countertransference as bedrock concepts of psychoanalytic therapy and a primary source of learning in therapy. Transference is the patient's emotional experience of and fantasies about the therapist which, though they may be based in part on actual perceptions of the therapist, recapitulate experience with and fantasies about important people in the patient's childhood (Person et al., 2005). Alternatively, some use a more general definition of the patient's emotional reactions toward the therapist (Colson, 1995). All manner of feelings held by the patient about the therapist might be considered transference. Transference interpretations focus on the relationship between patient and therapist. Countertransference refers to the therapist's emotional reactions to the patient and particularly reactions to the patient's transference, a kind of resonance with the patient. Transference allows the therapist and patient to make ordinarily unconscious thoughts and feelings conscious. as illustrated in the following vignette.

Let's look at an instance of the patient's anger and the therapist's responses. When angrily criticized by the patient for insensitivity the therapist may at first wonder if in fact he is letting the patient down, or he might feel counter-anger, or defensively remind himself that he is not such a bad guy as the patient may indicate. If there is a sufficient alliance so that both parties think further about their reactions, they consider that the patient tends to express anger initially formed with his father toward people in authority, like the therapist. The question arises for the therapist if he deserves that anger or whether the client is overreacting based on transference or both. The therapist shares this issue with the client and then they can collaboratively search for additional meanings together. Importantly the therapist does not respond as the father did by shutting the patient down. As they review this situation, the patient recalls how often he has been in trouble because of blowing up with bosses, supervisors, etc. The patient comments that never before has he been able to express anger without harsh negative consequences. This more benign realization may be a step on the way to better understanding problematic relationships.

Sometimes the client's anger with the therapist is due primarily to the therapist's behavior and is quite justified on that basis. Perhaps the therapist has been insensitive in which case it is a mistake for the therapist to trace the patient's anger to the father. In a defensive manner the therapist might deflect the client's anger away from himself, perhaps repeating the father's evasion. Unless caught and corrected such errors can damage trust in the therapist. Hopefully, the patient and therapist will work together to sort out a "misunderstanding". Eventually, the therapist sees his error, and thereby potential is created for an emotionally corrective experience in learning that anger can be expressed and worked out without escalation or retaliation.

Unconscious emotion

This next vignette illustrates the interplay of transference and countertransference.

The therapy with a moderately depressed middle-aged man dealt primarily with his stifled and largely unconscious feelings. He was a bright, likable, professional who seemed to long for love, an unacknowledged and unaware desire. It seemed that his longings were blocked by a rather harsh critical streak. His relationship with an adult son was a source of chronic disappointment. While he voiced yet another complaint among many criticisms about the son I felt a wave of sadness, an emotion seemingly not shared by the patient. Taking a clue from my response I decided to take a risk and asked "When was the last time you told your son you love him?" He suddenly burst into tears and sobbed for some time saying that he feared if he cried he would never stop. He later discussed a life-long prohibition about sharing tender feelings. When I asked him what it would be like for him if I were to express tender affectionate feelings for him he again responded with tears. This exchange of feeling marked a turning point in his therapy as though a curtain had been raised on a previously hidden part of his life.

Chapter 3

SYMPTOMS

The next three sections deal with symptoms of psychological disturbance. I wrote some about defenses in a prior chapter describing that defenses are a way to protect against pain. When our defenses fail the result is increased pain and we then must then resort to more extreme measures, which we view as symptoms. There are so many forms of symptoms it is impossible to list them but they all have in common a protective function and that they have meaning. Our unconscious efforts to protect ourselves against pain fail when problems accumulate beyond our capacity to contain, control or transform them into a more benign experience. Perhaps the underlying problems are too burdensome, too many or our capacities too compromised to work well for us. I will select what seem to me to be the most common categories of symptomatology for discussion. We could look at more specific symptoms like phobias, sexual dysfunction, interpersonal conflict, somatic complaints without physical cause, obsessive rituals, but many of these will be discussed in three general categories of symptoms: Depression, Anxiety and Panic, Post Traumatic Stress.

A. Depression can be intolerably painful

I will review some of the most frequent forms of suffering for which people seek psychotherapy namely, depression, anxiety, and traumatic stress. Depression, the topic of this segment, is somewhat different depending on whether it is part of a clinically significant disorder, is a so-called major depression, or is part of bipolar disorder. It is by far the most frequent factor in people seeking help though for some only time in therapy may reveal the basic depressive issue. The patient may seek help with alcoholism or some other form of addiction (there are many) not fully realizing that such symptoms are a flight from depression. And patients often discover that depression underlies a host of other presenting problems: sexual dysfunction, bodily complaints, marital conflict, anger outbursts.

Depression is likely to have a genetic component. This is not to say that depression is caused by genetic disposition. The genetic predisposition is likely to vary in influence in different people. It is particularly prominent in depressive people who are labeled bipolar. Those who claim that depression is solely biological do us a disservice by minimizing how much we can relieve depression or even eliminate it through psychological means. On the other hand, it is equally important to take predisposition seriously. It is more accurate to think, not in terms of cause, but more of predisposition with unknown influences.

To appreciate the suffering of severely depressed people one must understand that depression can result in excruciating, unbearable pain. The depressed person may feel depleted, drained, bereft, without energy, lacking internal resources. Some episodes of depression quickly pass and others in which the depression is more deeply entrenched will be long lasting. For serious depression treatment is essential, usually a combination of psychotherapy and medication, sometimes in conjunction with other treatments like family therapy, diet, exercise regimens, light therapy. For some patients medication may not be necessary but an influence is the risk that if the patient is not prescribed medication, some third parties may view that as neglect and might become a potential cause for liability.

It is helpful for a professional to guide the person through the sometimes perplexing array of options for help. Partly that is where a detailed diagnosis can be particularly relevant. Seeking help is still stigmatized in some quarters. Much of the time the patient has not sought help until depressive problems have accumulated to a point that the situation has become severe. Needing help sometimes confirms the depressed person's depressive ideas; that they are weak, can not cope on their own, that they are "sick". They may experience the need for help as cause for shame and humiliation.

Depression leads to a difficult to reverse dire state of mind when we have not been able to recognize a mounting number of stresses, miseries, often a bunch combined. It may seem that life is becoming increasingly burdensome; relationships are eroding, you are feeling guilty about some real or imagined misdeeds. Current deprivation may be stirring painful early childhood issues; you suffer from being abandoned or reactivation of trauma. Perhaps you have developed a serious illness or been seriously injured in love. Sometimes advancing age can be depressing (I speak from experience).

In those examples above at least some of the precipitants are obvious. When unable to recognize the stresses that are weighing on us we may flail about and send more or less disguised distress signals, as a ship that has gone on the rocks, sends an SOS in the hope someone out there will hear. The messages may take the form of anxiety attacks or behavior that is atypical for the person. For example, a sudden inexplicable affair, turning to drugs, alcohol, or risky behavior, becoming withdrawn and reclusive, having angry outbursts and heightened irritability, developing physical symptoms for which no physical cause can be found. It is worth noting that depression may predispose people to an array of physical problems. It is widely documented to have an adverse influence on the immune system.

Most people who suffer from depressive symptoms do not consider self-destructive behavior, but naturally depression increases the risk of such behavior, including the development of thoughts about suicide as a solution to severe emotional pain. The subject of suicide often frightens people and is treated as a taboo topic. However, it is likely that most people have thought about suicide at one point or another in their lives. I will assume that you are made of sturdy stuff and will tolerate my suggesting that any time the issue arises you should thoroughly discuss it in your therapy. Suicidal thoughts are the ultimate cry of despair and deserve our full attention. The depressed person may experience an acute neediness, intense longings for time, attention and nurturance, like a drowning person grasps for anything to hold onto, potentially another cause for shame. They may have never learned that we all need caring, interested and affirming others. They likely have an early history of emotional deprivation which when one is depressed will be reactivated.

While all the above is relevant a too exclusive focus on the patients pain and suffering may serve as rationalization by the patient and therapist for avoiding exploration of suicidal ideas in more detail. The discussion above misses some of the meaning of suicidal fantasies. That is that such thoughts contain and express anger. I will mention as episode reported to me by a colleague.

> A woman who had been abused in childhood is accused by a store clerk of stealing a CD of a movie. She was then subjected to the humiliating, intrusive experience of being searched revealing that she had not stolen anything. Later in her next therapy session she told her therapist that she was thinking of killing herself. Her therapist said that she was not comfortable with anger and she really wanted to kill that "bitch of a store clerk" who abused and humiliated her. The repetition of abuse in the present came too close to recreating her abuse as a child.

The point I wish to make is that too often our exploration of suicidal thinking ends prematurely with what seems most obvious because of our anxiety about suicidality.

Another not so obvious point about depression: The experience of a clinical depression shakes up one's internal status quo. That shaking up of ones internal life means that as the patient processes the depression, it's causes and messages, a reorganization is possible such that the patient may come out of the depression a changed person. Those changes are far more likely to be positive when the patient processes the relevant issues in therapy. Perhaps he emerges from his depression with a new found understanding of human suffering and capacity for empathy.

B. Anxiety and Panic

Anxiety may be ongoing or intermittent at mild moderate or severe levels. In part because anxiety is accompanied by high levels of mental and physical activation it may result in physical symptoms such as high blood pressure, gastro-intestinal distress, hypertension, headaches. Without intervention, at some point the physical symptoms of anxiety may result in serious illnesses. It is commonly understood that anxiety and stress take a toll on the immune system. Anxiety tends to have a contagious quality. In my clinical experience, anxious parents tend to have anxious children. The anxious person may irritate others because they tend to be controlling. It is as though they think that if they can control the world around them all would be well with less cause for anxiety. To assess the prevalence of anxiety, think of the people you know, perhaps including yourself, who seem fearful, tense, report phobias as in fear of heights, have nightmares, seem overly cautious or overprotective, are fidgety and "nervous", wring their hands, exude distress, frequently sigh deeply.

When traumatic or disturbing feelings, worries, events, or thoughts accumulate beyond our capacity to contain them we feel overwhelmed and may become unable to function. Panic attacks are a signal that our defenses are failing, pressures are becoming too great, and may threaten a collapse of our ability to function. The anxiety attack says that I have too much on my emotional plate and measures must be taken to reduce the pressure. A panic attack is accompanied by physiological arousal; flushing, difficulty catching one's breath, hyperventilation, a feeling of imminent doom, the sensation of an enormous weight on one's chest. Once you have experienced one you are unlikely to forget it. Leading up to it may be an accumulation of stresses; conflicts with a spouse, the job is increasingly stressful, a parent recently died. The anxiety attack announces a dire state of mind and hopefully, we can listen to what it is telling us. The panic experienced is akin to the distress of suddenly looking up to see a train bearing down on you.

Too often concern is solely with the panic we have been experiencing and less with it's message. The message may be to reduce one's work load, to work on conflict in the marriage, to find ways to alleviate one's worries, in effect to take measures to reduce pressures on oneself. Often the person is relatively unaware of the stresses which are the culprit. We can't change what we don't know or understand. Psychotherapy may help increase self awareness. In my experience the patient's anxiety decreases to some extent not long after beginning therapy. Perhaps for some people the experience of a therapist's availability, concern and interest are sufficient to reassure and reduce some pain.

A part of the message delivered by the panic attack may be that a clinical depression is just around the corner. Depression's onset is often gradual with the person's failing to recognize the accumulation of troubles or how serious a toll depression may take on the ability to live day-to-day life and indeed on the ability to survive. Once depression seems to be approaching a critical mass it is essential that the person get psychological help, perhaps including psychotherapy and medication. This is one of the times in life when it is particularly important to resist the need to isolate oneself and instead engage with caring others, perhaps friends and family.

C. Post traumatic stress is pervasive

Most people likely suffer from some posttraumatic stress, the kind experienced in the usual course of life events: for a sudden significant loss or separation, a severe blow to one's self-esteem, an auto accident, a relationship crisis as in divorce, a move of residence, some illnesses, medical procedures. Any experience that results in an extreme sense of helplessness that one is overwhelmed can be considered trauma. So there are many more instances of post-traumatic stress in our lives than is commonly appreciated. Based on clinical experience with severely traumatized people there are many ways, including educational efforts, to help traumatized people understand their condition and the consequences of traumatization(Allen, 2001). Trauma may effect not only your psychological and social development but also your physiological functioning. A group experience may be useful for traumatized people in-so-far as they may learn that most reactions to trauma are natural.

Stresses may be accompanied by minor interference in daily living but to be classified as a disorder they must have a significant influence on one's life, interference with the ability to function. Some examples would be: following an auto accident, for a long time, the person is too disturbed to drive, after a terrible divorce, for years the person avoids potentially romantic relationships, following a major move of residence nightmares about the move recur for many months and frequently disturb sleep and then the well known PTSD which may occur during and after time in the military.

The flashbacks or sudden intrusive reappearance of trauma can so disrupt daily life as to render the person nonfunctional.

> As another example, let's consider trauma following a serious auto accident. The driver was stopped ready to turn left into a parking lot. He had a second's glimpse of a truck in his rear view mirror before the world exploded. The next thing he knew he was lying in the back seat looking up at the roof. People were soon talking to him, but he could not understand them. It just sounded like noise. There were sirens and after a while he was pulled from the car by rescue folks and then ambulanced to the nearest emergency room. He never felt anything, any fear or pain, just numbness. After a half day in a hospital, he was assured there was no serious physical damage, aside from a few bruises and some whiplash. Within a few days to a couple of weeks later he found that getting in a car terrified him. That fear diminished over a few weeks and then he was compelled to repeatedly look in the rear view mirror. For some time after the accident, he was quite irritable and sometimes inexplicably tearful. Any loud noise would evoke a marked startle reaction. In his therapy, he reviewed frightening events occurring since his childhood. Trauma, like significant losses, operates like a tuning fork with multiple tines wherein each resonates with all others. So a single traumatic episode is seldom felt as only that but instead reactivates the responses to all prior disturbing events. This factor, the resonance of one trauma with all others, partly explains why achieving recovery takes significant time.

There is a misconception that terrible life events will inevitably result in PTSD. This is not the case. Some people seem to have relatively less proneness to suffer from PTSD than others. Those who are at increased risk are people who are vulnerable because of mental illness or those who have suffered from previous debilitating PTSD. The major sources of childhood trauma may be verbal or physical abuse, sexual abuse, abandonment, neglect or deprivation of essential supplies and are likely to predispose to trauma later in life. That is, people who have been significantly traumatized early in life will be more vulnerable to trauma later.

There have been long-standing debates among mental health professionals about reports of childhood neglect and abuse. How literally should one hear a person's description of childhood trauma? Might such reports be mistaken or misrepresent the facts? But for the most part regardless of doubts about specific events, where there is smoke there is fire. That is, there is usually some basis for reports of abuse and neglect. Frequently people who report sexual abuse have been met with doubt, skepticism and occasional accusations of outright lying. When such cases go to court it is typical for the traumatized person to be re-traumatized by court proceedings and often enough the court is vicariously traumatized as well. It is likely that juries and other members of the court will sometimes be traumatized by some of the horror stories heard as part of court proceedings.

An especially problematic situation is where the person, on the basis of present symptoms (promiscuity or an aversion to sex), strongly suspects that they were abused in childhood but have no memory, or at best a few fragments that might suggest abuse. They may experience so-called flashbacks to the early abuse consisting of disturbing bodily sensations, unwelcome recollections, odors, visual images of abuse or other fragments of the experience. For example, a person responds to caresses with an experience of being abusively touched. Or they may experience touch as irritating and intrusive rather than affectionate. Perhaps they can not tolerate anyone moving close. One of my patients would experience sudden overwhelming anxiety when exposed to certain odors. She couldn't explain this occurrence. We discovered after a time that the odors are of the pastries the abuser would give her to buy her compliance.

Abuse may occur in anyone's life and accompany any diagnostic features. A few specific treatments have been proposed as effective with trauma (EMDR or systematic desensitization). From my experience I have come to believe that therapy may hold as much or more promise of long-term relief than any of those specialized treatments. If patient and therapist decide to take on severe trauma they may may be in for a rough ride.

One of my severely abused patients in dissociative reliving of aspects of her abuse would stand up, move to a corner of my office, whimper. cry, plead with me to not hurt her and sometimes scream. Over time such episodes became less frequent and as I set some gentle limits, she seemed a bit more in control and less panicky. She was re-experiencing the terror of the trauma in a safe setting and thereby gradually reducing it's toxicity. She was helped by my reminding her of how much she could be in control in her life and I encouraged her to recognize the strong will she could demonstrate.

Chapter 4

STAGES OF THERAPY

A. The experience of beginning

The therapy starts with two people meeting and interacting, each with their strengths and vulnerabilities. The therapist helped by his skills and knowledge will have needs and limitations that he will modulate and process for the sake of shared goals. The patient typically arrives in a vulnerable state of mind, looking for help with suffering, pain and holds distinctive expectations and hopes. The therapist has knowledge of guidelines for proceeding and how the mind works. The therapist will aim first to help establish a safe atmosphere and then will gradually apply his knowledge to provide relief of symptoms, new learning, and new perspectives.

In early sessions, it is useful for the patient to have an opportunity to state understandable anxiety. One might expect to feel some uncomfortable self-consciousness. After all, you are about to share some personal matters with a relative stranger. You and your therapist will develop a series of agreements (a contract) outlining fees, methods of payment, insurance issues, frequency and times of appointments, confidentiality and its limits. Typically, the therapist will explain that exceptions to confidentiality may occur if the patient poses a significant danger to himself or others.

Also in the beginning there is a tendency, as in many other relationships, for the patient to idealize the therapist. This initially may be looked on as a favorable tendency as it facilitates the development of a working alliance and is an aid to the client's involvement in the therapy. As with all idealizations gradually a period of disenchantment follows. This shift is a natural process that tends to bring patients losses to the forefront, ushering in a middle phase, a period of ascending depressive concerns.

It will be helpful for you to be aware that, if you have insurance, you have authorized the insurance company to have access to your clinical information. They will, at a minimum, require your therapist to provide a diagnostic label, sometimes much more. I have known of instances in which the patient has been denied health insurance because of a prior history of being in therapy. If these exceptions to confidentiality are unavoidable, pay out of pocket, if you can. For some therapists, the fee may be negotiable. Also, beware if, for payment, the therapist takes a chicken, a work of art or a valuable Persian rug. Don't laugh. I have heard of some even more bizarre arrangements! While bartering is not necessarily an ethical violation, it brings complicated motives to the therapy for both parties and may lead to a suspicion of exploitation.

First impressions are important, the therapist's manner and appearance, the waiting room and office, the welcome of a receptionist. We should train our secretarial and billing staff in aspects of courtesy and kindness. In discussing the "contract" therapy, has begun. Thoughts and feelings relevant to your problems may very well emerge in these discussions. For example, if you tend to be withholding and tight with a nickel that will likely affect the fee discussion. That "frugal" streak may lead to other issues, such as the influence on your other relationships, not feeling worthy or doubting the value of the therapist's services.

Many patients have little idea of what therapy is about, how it is conducted and what may be expected of them. So you might look to your therapist to provide some education about these issues. And that may be helpful at many junctures. For example, when the therapist first asks the patient his thoughts and feelings about the therapist the patient may be puzzled, sometimes resentful. After all, the client may think, the therapy is supposed to be about me, not about the therapist. I might then explain that therapy is in some ways different than most doctor-patient relationships. That is, feelings and thoughts about the therapist, particularly those bearing on trust, may influence the patient's use the therapy, so it is important to have an opportunity to discuss such thoughts.

B. Initiating a process of inquiry

First and foremost psychotherapy should be characterized by inquiry and exploration (Lichtenberg, 2005). For that spirit to flourish it is important to develop at atmosphere of trust. If you can come to feel respected, a significant step has been taken. Then the process will evolve as seed in a fertile field. If you meet a therapist who exclaims "trust me," you might give that threapist a second thought. Confidence in a therapist, or anyone else for that matter, should be earned, not given. If not, you make yourself blind. Also, remember that there has never been, nor will there ever be, a person exactly like you. Your uniqueness means that you will have your individualized course of therapy. Also, you can know from the outset that a one size fits all therapy(as in the use of standardized manuals) will be quite limited.

At first the therapist is likely to start with an open-ended question like "how can I help you" or "tell me about what brings you to therapy"? In the beginning, issues you do not spontaneously discuss the therapist will likely ask about. Your moods, present life circumstances, including any self-destructive ideas or actions. Useful information will also come from inquiry about gratifications, sources of happiness or unhappiness, symptoms, how your symptoms developed, your fears, hopes and ambitions and details about your significant relationships. If any of these topics is too emotionally difficult to address in the present, don't hesitate to say so. Most can be deferred to a more comfortable time.

The therapist might want to hear about details of your early years and your views about how aspects of childhood affect you now. You may not see any reason to discuss childhood as your problems are in the present. The therapist might affirm this view that it is important to look in detail at the present and explain that in a further discussion you may find that some childhood events help to explain the present. Also, in beginning, it is typical, at least unconsciously, for patients to expect and fear that unfortunate events in other relationships will be repeated with the therapist. You will discover, over time, that this occurrence, the repetition of some of your problems in the therapy, is a natural part of the process. It provides access to work on your relationship problems. Your assumptions about the therapist or therapy are best made explicit and examined. Some such potentially distorted assumptions may be that therapists are inordinately interested in childhood, sex, or money.

Most topics will be reviewed many times, over extended periods of time. You will likely find that, no matter how many times you discuss a problem, there is something new in each recounting. So there is a reason for covering the same territory over and over. No matter what concern arises, you may benefit from discussing it with the therapist. The technical words for this process of repetition allowing expansion and deepening of insight is "working through."

In the beginning patients will frequently fear that they will be found boring, blamed for whatever problem they experience, criticized and accused of "badness" in one form or another. The therapist should ask about your reactions to him, particularly critical ones. Sometimes, to test whether they should trust the therapist, a patient will be provocative and then be attentive to how the therapist reacts, looking for signs of retaliation, punitive reactions or vulnerability.

On one occasion a patient, blessed with a spectacular figure, arrived for her first appointments wearing a skimpy low cut blouse and shockingly short skirt. I do not know if there was a "wow" reaction discernable in my demeanor but I think that I kept my typical composure, with a bit of effort. Later it turned out that this young woman was sexually abused in childhood. She was earning money through prostitution. She left therapy after four sessions without paying the bill.

Another client a middle aged lawyer, in our first sessions took voluminous, verbatim notes, without any mention of doing so, which I found a bit unnerving. I asked if note taking was an important part of his occupation, which transitioned into a discussion about his dissatisfaction with his law practice and a bit later his fear that he would, in various ways, loose control. His notes provided him some sense of being in control. So whatever your style of presentation it has its psychological and relationship function, even if you find yourself being provocative.

C. Timing is important

If you have a history of trauma, including childhood abuse, it should be explored but only to the extent that you will not recreate trauma in recalling the details. Sometimes telling the story of trauma will return to awareness the pain associated with the original events. If you say too much too soon about such potentially overwhelming memories and events, you may repeat being overwhelmed and traumatized. The time will likely come when the deferred details and associated feelings can and should be more safely explored. If a therapist pushes you to talk about trauma, like jumping in the deep end of the pool without prior discussion of risk, you may be wise to hesitate. Some clients will pressure themselves into tackling abuse prematurely hoping to get the pain behind them as soon as possible. Remember that, although the therapist encouraging exploration is generally helpful, there may be a better time and place and that you deserve respect for your unique timing.

Having emphasized the importance of timing it is also true that the success of therapy may rest on your willingness to reveal complicated thoughts, memories, and feelings, in the past and present. Your work in that direction is helped by the therapist's support and understanding. If that support is not forthcoming, that is also a worthy topic for discussion. The therapist might let the client know that a sense of safety is helpful but so is your together assembling explanations of your problems and there is tension between these two possibilities. For the client to discover that problematic issues do in fact have explanations may be a major beginning step and may enhance the patient's motivation.

D. Collaboration

Therapists working within a psychoanalytic model will, with one exception to be described further on, begin in the early phase introducing the client to the idea that the relationship between therapist and client is a valuable source of information. The therapist will initiate discussion of ways that your relationship (transference) may either facilitate or obstruct the therapy, more likely to be an obstruction when not discussed. The therapist may tell you that your coming to feel safe and comfortable is important and will help the work, so that obstacles to a sense of trust and safety should be discussed as soon as possible. There are some therapies in which there is little or no reference to or examination of the patient-therapist relationship, in consideration of the potentially overwhelming feelings that might be released in doing so. Exploration requires different tolerances and pacing for some patients than for others. Where the patient might be too uncomfortable with the closeness involved in speaking directly about the therapy relationship ample relationship information will come from discussion of relationships outside the therapy. Perhaps the crucial issue for outcome is the therapeutic alliance. The alliance, the extent of cooperation between patient and therapist, has been shown to be related to positive outcomes in therapy and perhaps attention to the collaboration will be the best predictor of improvement (Colson et al.,1988). So it may be useful for you to be attentive to how well you and the therapist seem to be working together and to discuss any problems.

Every therapist has an individual style and idiosyncracies, One of mine is that, when the patient precedes me into my office I imagine their stride like that of the child they once were, and in ways still are, an image that brings a smile. After all, our struggles as adults are not so far removed from those early days. What a pleasure it is for me to begin this voyage together with the patient, at moments taxing our patience, but overall a remarkable worthy adventure.

E. Facilitating change

Much of the facilitation of change in psychotherapy comes from the benign and supportive aspects of the patient-therapist relationship. This support includes courtesy, kindness, respect, positive regard for the patient, fondness, optimism about the capacity for change, and a nurturing attitude. It is important to remember that for the most part people appreciate feeling cared about. These attitudes are therapeutic, in part, because one can so seldom count on continuing kindness, nurturance and support in relationships. Such qualities because they underscore the patient's value, tend to have healing properties. In the history of the development of psychotherapy, we have come to emphasize that the personal human engagement between patient and therapist is of utmost importance.

This 'holding' aspect of therapy is most crucial in building what therapists call the therapeutic alliance, the positive collaboration between patient and therapist. Sometimes the single most useful contribution to a working partnership is the therapist's underscoring the value of the patient's observations and respect for the patient's acuity, hard work, intelligence, sensitivity, generosity. The alliance is the total of reasonable, cooperative, motivated qualities in the relationship in which two people work together to achieve shared aims and includes the patient's collaboration with the therapist. It may be worth noting, once again, that a positive working alliance is a powerful predictor of good therapy outcomes(Horwitz, et al, 2005).

The aspects of therapy I will discuss next are therapeutically useful in addition to the powerful influence of the factors above. I avoid the word "technique" and prefer language better fitting a human exchange. However, in this section I use a few technical phrases (e.g. transference and countertransference). This language plays a part in the therapists thinking and has become recognized in common parlance, and, as I define them, should be relatively easy to understand.

1. Listening and questioning: The most elementary steps are listening and questioning initiating a process of inquiry. Listening is far more than a passive process of attending to what the patient says. It also includes the therapist indicating that he is listening (yes, I see, uh huh, could you say a bit more), attending to related topics or meanings, hearing the range of emotion and emotional nuance. An enormous amount of information emerges directly from this mode of working, and it is the most frequent mode of interaction

Questioning is to help the patient elaborate, to take the subject further, an invitation, with each of the therapists questions conveying his active listening and interest in the patient. Many people will have never experienced this degree of close attention before, an experience that may be either frightening or therapeutic in itself.

> One patient who was new to therapy exclaimed how remarkable it was to experience attention to her, as she had never experienced before. It made her nervous to

think I was taking her seriously. Perhaps I was looking for something about her thinking or behavior to criticize. Soon she was questioning why her family had never seemed to listen or take her seriously. Now this does not mean the therapist hovers; rather he is attentive in ways that underscore that the patient is worth listening to.

I think of inquiry opening a door along a path to further exploration. Opening doors to a new territory can be frightening as well as gratifying, and you should take ample time to discuss those reactions. When efforts to inquire and elaborate are met with resistance (perhaps prolonged silences) may be when patience is needed and later understanding of the reasons for hesitation will be useful.

2. Confronting and clarifying Much of the therapist's activity will be in clarifying and confronting something the patient has said. So when the patient refers to having drunk "a little too much" last night the therapist might ask," you mean that you got drunk!" or "could you be minimizing the amount of drinking?" Or when the patient describes a bitter argument with his wife the therapist may say "It seems that, unfortunately, hurt feelings were inflicted on both sides." Or "perhaps you underestimate the importance and weight that others give to what you say. Sometimes a confrontation shows concern by in spirit exclaiming:" OK, let's quit soft-pedaling, and get real."

3. Interpretation: Another therapist activity called interpretation consists of statements by the therapist with an intent to explain. "I wonder if that argument was made worse by yesterday's difference in opinion about how to manage the children?" Sometimes interpretation is referred to as implicitly containing a "because clause" with the therapist suggesting a causal connection between two concerns, feelings, or events. Might you be angry with your wife "because", yesterday, she touched a sensitive place and offended you?" Each new connection made by the therapist and patient potentially extends understanding of the patient's struggles and deepens the patients thinking. Interpretations in a cumulative manner emphasize connections between different realms of experience and thereby gradually broaden and deepen perspectives. This work has

the potential to make conscious what has been unconscious. For some people insight may proceed too quickly and the patient will respond with opposition or increased anxiety. Pacing is best discussed, a discussion which in itself may result in a significant benefit and improved collaboration between patient and therapist. The therapist might ask if the patient thinks that they are moving too fast.

4. Transference and countertransference interpretation: These interventions focus on the relationship between the patient and therapist. Countertransference refers to the therapist's emotional reactions to the patient and particularly reactions to the patient's transference. These reactions of patient and therapist to one another are crucial to an understanding psychoanalytic therapy. These variables were previously discussed in Chapter one. But some further elaboration might be in order. Therapies that on balance seem supportive with very little or no interpretive work are called "supportive." While those with more interpretive emphasis are called "expressive." The choice of interventions is complicated. With a group of colleagues, we took ten years to study which interventions were preferable for each of three borderline patients (Horwitz et al, 2005). Those researchers underscored that supportiveness and expressiveness are not a single continuum but two dimensions. So therapy can be both supportive and expressive.

Let's look at another transference-countertransference situation. The therapist falls asleep in a session. If the therapist is defensive about the patient's understandable annoyance an opportunity may be lost. The therapists first response might be to offer a genuine apology, without which you may be unwilling to engage in further exploration. Then learning may be possible, for example, whether you tend to avoid conflict, perhaps pretending not to notice the therapist's lapse. Do you feel worthy of the therapist's full attention, linked to a self esteem issue. Do you attack the therapist as all bad without redeeming qualities, perhaps allowing recognition of polarizations in your views of others. Might you understandably scold the therapist revealing a sense of yourself as having value? There are many avenues for exploration and learning. Of course if the sleeping episode is repeated you have cause to explore whether you should find a different therapist.

5. Working through: Psychotherapy includes much repetition. It is repetition in endless variations on each contribution to each symptom which is the best guarantee that the changes in psychotherapy can be long lasting. Only by examining the many ways a problem is manifested does the patient comes to thoroughly recognize the role of that problem, in his internal life and relationships. For example, a patient will review his self defeating aggression as it appears in the family, at work, in friendships, with men and women, in therapy and back again to each of those contexts. With each repetition there are new elements, a new emphasis, a new perspective. all leading to an expanding, deepening, and better integrated comprehension of oneself.

The factors that follow focus on qualities of the relationship and have a more modern development. They are simultaneously experiences and abilities that at the beginning of therapy forecast good outcomes and that in the course of psychotherapy may grow and benefit the process. To help you understand these qualities I will describe each to convey some of what you may experience in therapy.

6. Enactment refers to an interaction between therapist and patient in which together you unwittingly play out some dysfunctional interaction from the past, analogous to the transference-countertransference discussion above. This interplay will serve as a source of learning for both parties. The reason this is important is that the interaction as an enactment becomes a convincing illustration of a relationship problem, an example of a problematic relationship pattern. Let's look at an example.

> The client's parents were overworked, over worried people who were afraid to let their child out of their sight. The patient became accustomed to this hovering style of relationship in childhood, and as he matured, he came to create and then resent that kind of relationship. In therapy sessions, he discussed his wish to move forward in his career but did so accompanied by a description of various catastrophes that might result. For instance, he could not tolerate the possibility of failing, his boss would resent his ambition, he might not be as available

to his ailing parents, others would see him as selfish. The therapist found himself responding to the patient with a note of worried caution. He wondered if the patient was moving ahead too fast or too soon. Without conscious awareness, he was slowing the patient and conveying anxiety about the patients steps forward. Finally, the patient complained about the therapist discouraging him. The therapist recognized and discussed his role in the replay of the patient's contradictory feelings. He could then show the patient how he unconsciously invited others to worry about him, as with his parents. He then experienced others as anxiously holding him back instead of recognizing and dealing with his anxiety and fearfulness.

7. Mentalization: A relatively recent concept is called metallization and might be closely related to another idea of mindfulness from the field of meditation. Mentalizing, among various meanings, refers to your ability to recognize your and others' mental states. This ability typically improves in therapy. It refers to a process, a result, and a marker of change. Imagine trying to get by in life unable to identify your needs and wants and those of others. When the therapist asks for elaboration of your thoughts and feelings or another's thoughts and feelings the groundwork is set for examining what interferes with the ability to mentalize, what gets in the way of being able to know about such matters. Did you come from a family in which no one talked about meaningful topics, nor was such expression valued? Were questions about thoughts and feelings discouraged? When you showed a feeling were you quickly turned off. Did you live with circumstances that killed curiosity? Was the expression of anger equated with violence? In fact, if one can develop an interest in what others feel you have come a long way toward preventing insensitive behavior. Growing up in a suffocating, action dominated, non-reflective atmosphere could partly explain the lack of mentalizing. In fact, the mental activity of reflection, as in being able to think about oneself and others is closely related, if not identical, to being able to mentalize.

I worked with a person whose capacity for reflection or mentalizing was minimal. When we were first together in my office, and I did not conform to his expectations he glared at me in such an intense angry way I felt afraid. When kept waiting for someone he could not imagine a reason for their lateness, or their mental state, and could only ragefully think of "ripping their head off" as he put it. He was similarly infuriated in most frustrating circumstances, and he seldom failed to tell off the offending person or found some way to retaliate. Over years of therapy, he was never late for our appointments. When exploring this intolerance he could not imagine why anyone might behave differently than he. When selecting a woman to date he was unable to pick up on clues she would drop about herself. He could not hear them or attend to their meaning. So with women he was always blindsided.

I knew we were making progress when after years of therapy we could talk about different points of view without his tense anger looming. He could allow himself to be a bit late to a session now and then. Accompanying that change, there was a slight incremental increase in his ability to know what another person might be thinking or feeling. Over the years we worked together we formed strong bonds of affection. None-the-less when his anger was stirred it was difficult for him to call on his new capacity. He aptly described himself as born in a "half-cocked" position

8. Psychological Mindedness. Now we will consider a mental capacity that may develop over the course of psychotherapy, akin to mentalizing and reflection. Psychological Mindedness is the ability to alternate between feelings and reflecting about them, openly expressing oneself and observing the meaning and significance of that expression. This capacity requires an ability to think abstractly, to be able to see the similarities between different realms of experience. To the extent that psychological mindedness gains a foothold in the patient's thinking, it will be of enormous help in the subsequent therapy. Mentalizing, reflection, and psychological mindedness are so closely related in

meaning; not much is gained by belaboring this one. It is fairly often that a person begins therapy with little idea of the importance of these abilities. As experience is gained with exploration and interpretation the ability increases, one of the major indicators that treatment is progressing well. Some people are unable to make significant gains in this area because of deficits, perhaps an organic brain component as in a severe Attention Deficit Hyperactivity Disorder (ADHD). If you seem stuck in building these capacities, you may benefit from discussing the implications with your therapist.

9. Spontaneity and Intimacy. There are many references in the psychotherapy literature to spontaneous happenings, moments of meeting as called by one author. I have noted that many people who have been in therapy report that one of their most meaningful and positive exchanges with the therapist being when they joined in laughter. These cumulative experiences, as much as any previously mentioned, are markers of forward movement and a deepening of the patient-therapist relationship. To be sufficiently at ease to allow such moments of spontaneity is a positive indicator for the course of therapy.

Another period of intimacy comes to mind that had a profound impact on the patient. A depressed isolated lonely elderly man was recounting some early childhood memories, including one from around the age of six. He lived with his parents and younger sister on a ground level of an apartment building in a large city. He recalled times during the heat of summer when the milkman left clinking glass bottles on the front porch and the iceman would haul giant blocks of ice on his back up two flights of stairs. The therapist added to the memory that in those sweltering days the children take pieces of ice off the back of the truck. This comment resonated with the patient's "private" early memory, with resulting tears and relief in feeling less alone. These comments were only possible because of the therapists early memories, that happened to parallel those of the patient.

I have seen many occasions in which particularly poignant contacts between patient and therapist occur, a delight to experience and an indicator of therapy going well.

10. Empathy. The patient learns to appreciate the inner world and experience of the other, in part, by experiencing the therapist entering the patient's internal life and points of view. The development of empathy is one of the most significant gains for the person in psychotherapy. It is particularly rewarding to both client and therapist to experience improved empathic skills in a previously unfeeling patient, perhaps one who has been beset with narcissistic limitations. Perhaps for the patient in the distant past an empathic stance had come to mean a too vulnerable undefended state of mind. The very guarded person may be afraid to be so receptive. One analyst describes that in order to "find" the patient we must look for him in ourselves (Bollas,1987). I have heard stories from others about patients who come out of therapy increasingly comfortable with offensive character problems as in being less receptive, more guarded, more insensitive, but I have not seen a single instance.

F. The long Mid-Phase

Every process has a beginning middle and end, as does a course of psychotherapy. These three phases each has its own themes. The beginning is full of anticipation, hopefulness, looking forward, sometimes with a near magical sense of possibilities. The middle is the phase of endurance, maturation of themes, pulling together of previously fragmented feelings, thoughts, or memories and a dawning realization that nothing is forever and therapy like stories, movies, plays and life will some day come to a conclusion.

By now the patient realizes that certain problematic aspects of his life and relationships are deeply embedded, and that he plays a role in creating problems, which before seemed to him to be part of his destiny or somehow developed without his participation. When therapy has gone well this mid-phase can be a time of disenchantment, an end to the hope that problems will be resolved magically or without effort or that everything is resolvable.

The relationship between the therapist and patient is now one of the most important aspects of the patient's life. Interactions between them will be saturated with meaning for the patient, attached to therapist lateness, absences, real or imagined slights. Often with new learning about oneself comes an awkwardness and surprise. One's sense of self may be shaken, like a centipede thinking how it walks and becomes all trips and stumbles. These heightened sensitivities provide a productive field for the exploration of interpersonal problems. The ongoing focus may be on relations with children, a marriage or relationship with a significant other. One may come to appreciate, through the therapy, that relationships are the most crucial defining parts of life and that pain about them is not completely resolvable. We are embedded in an evolving life long matrix of relationships which define us, give us direction and through which we create meaning.

For a number of years, therapists have felt increasingly free to share some personal reactions with their patients, occasionally including feelings about the patient. Therapist "neutrality" had, for a long time, meant that therapists should not express feelings about patients. The trend toward more therapist transparency is a welcome one. Patients should gradually come to know that therapists are human beings with their own thoughts, needs, and feelings. And the therapist will now acknowledge that aspects of therapy are to satisfy the therapist's needs; to see that he has a comfortable work space, the fee and aspects of the schedule.

Patients may feel stuck for significant periods of time, unable to return to what used to define them, because that has changed, and unable to move forward into an unknown future. We are creatures of habit and the familiar is more comfortable than unknowns. The therapist will be alert to hopes, aspirations, new recognitions and scenarios, small steps forward, analogous to the understanding that if a pup, is nurtured, it will eventually grow into his big feet. Sometimes, in the patient's involvement in the therapy, he may have difficulty recognizing those small steps as representing progress.

> Let's consider examples: A woman, as a result of the building of trust and comfort, and other preparatory work of the first phase, had recently begun talking about details of early sexual abuse. Then hesitantly, showing much shame, she revealed new information about promiscuity in her young adult years and that

currently she had no sexual feelings or excitement in her marriage. As a child she was threatened by her abuser with harm and harm to the family if she discussed her abuse with anyone. Terrified, she talked to no one and consequently remained frozen, locked in an experience of fear, helplessness, shame, and self hatred. The therapist commented on the courage required to begin discussing this painful chapter in her life and that she was taking a positive step, particularly considering that she was afraid that I would shame and punish her. Her early promiscuity was all action and little feeling, an effort to regain a sense of control. She became convinced, correctly I think, that the details of abuse would have to be discussed in detail, perhaps repeatedly, to allow her greater emotional freedom.

A man in his 20s, while bright, could not be articulate and was full of self doubt, often stumbling over his words preventing him from pursuing goals and showing any assertiveness. In his relatively long term attendance of group and individual therapy this meek and self-effacing man was gradually able to express criticism and anger toward the therapist. It was particularly useful for the group to witness the emergence of these previously hidden aspect of the fellow. We explored together the experiences which had caused him to become so beaten down. The accepting group and non critical and non defensive demeanor of the therapist, along with insight, into the role of his intimidating father, provided a crucial corrective experience. His finely honed critical ability could not begin to emerge, nor his considerable capacity for affection, without the initial phase of increasing trust and confidence and some explanations of the reasons for his inhibitions in the area of exercising critical ability.

Another patient in a prolonged beginning stage talked about his mother's serious instability. She was fragile, psychotic (out of touch with reality), frequently flew into rages and was probably delusional about the father. The beginning of a middle stage was marked by a dream of his mother as a hologram, expressing a new awareness that, as one would create a hologram, he created his mother in the present, one of the ways being to marry an extremely disturbed woman.

Perhaps you can recognize from these examples these patient's pursuit of steps toward wholeness, agency (the sense of being initiator), new meaning, the integration of past with present, and greater psychological health.

G. Ending as a blessing and curse

This discussion of the ending phase of therapy rests on the premise that ending is not as a discrete action but rather is a more or less extended process. Summing up, reviewing and integrating the work of the preceding therapy and saying goodbye take time. How do we know when it is time to anticipate an end to therapy? There is no one time when termination is timely; rather it is thinkable to consider at various junctures throughout the therapy. If you raise the subject very early, then we might consider whether something impels you to take flight. This is the time when quitting should not be an option, at least until you discuss the problematic issue. You may be on the verge of a particularly important, but anxiety arousing, topic when quitting becomes hard to resist.

A patient began therapy without revealing his fear of being shamed by the therapist. After a few sessions, he quit without discussion with the therapist because of that fear. He simply didn't show up for subsequent sessions. As is frequently the case in such abrupt endings, I wrote a letter to the patient expressing my concern about his sudden disappearance adding a question about whether I had offended him in some way and expressed my wish that he return if only for a single meeting. The patient revealed the problem in the subsequent session. It is a disappointment to the therapist when there is no opportunity to discuss the problematic issue and the patient is short-changed. In most cases when the patient can make their reservations known they can be worked out. A few reasons for premature endings include fear of criticism or of being humiliated, unexplored worries about money, wishing to "leave well enough alone", or dissatisfaction with the therapist. My experience indicates that the more the patient has been immersed in the therapy, the more time might be required for ending.

A major theme of this period tends to be endings. All manner of endings are re-experienced and explored: influential separations and losses including lost friendships and loves, deaths of those who are, or have been significant. The ending may facilitate a resumption of prematurely interrupted grieving

> One middle-aged fellow had a recurrence of longing for a first love and sadness about the traumatic way that the relationship had ended many years before. I encouraged him to think about and say now to the previously lost person what he wished he had said but did not when he had the chance. Similarly the patient might voice feelings toward someone who has died. The results of saying the unsaid are often poignant and moving. The process of ending might help the patient recover the full range and depth of feeling for lost relationships, including regret, and then, perhaps, some degree of letting go may follow.

Sometimes the patient expresses considerable disappointment that in the therapy certain goals are not attained or only partially so, in the manner of "I never promised you a rose garden." The therapist may or may not reveal that he harbors similar reservations. Along with gratitude, some disappointment is inevitable, also part of the termination process(Greenberg, 2015). After all, one of the most intimate relationships in the patient's life is about to end. Giving up the luxury of attention devoted exclusively to you is also a loss. For most it's hard to say goodbye, and ending may be not so easy to celebrate, underscoring the natural limits to everything.

When it comes to physical contact, hugs and more, which are likely to occur naturally near an ending, the therapist may clarify what he does, or he doesn't do and explain the reasons or the limited circumstances when a hug, for instance, might be OK. There are certain stated longings, including sexual ones that should be discussed, helped by the therapist's comfortable confidence that he will never indulge such wishes, during or after therapy. The subject of contact with one another outside therapy, likely to arise at termination, is a sensitive one and potential for the patient feeling rejected. Therapists should be respectful of the sensitivities involved while avoiding being unnecessarily severe or withholding. During this ending phase, it is common that reciprocal caring feelings are expressed. On occasion, I will meet with a patient for coffee and chat after a while following termination. If you are an inhibited person you may have a fantasy that such contacts with the therapist are forbidden. I would urge you to explore those thoughts with your therapist. If you do so you may discover the fearfulness and inhibition in your relationships in large part are self imposed.

Sometimes setting a termination date stirs a realization that the date is premature and that much remains to be discussed. Termination may then be postponed until a more satisfactory time. Fears may arise for the patient of being without the therapists help. The client may feel that there is no need at the moment but wishes to hold onto the therapist as a kind of insurance, that is if something urgent arises the therapist will still be there. Then some patients will renew complaints about some aspect of their work or relationships in the hope that patient and therapist will then recognize that the present is no time to discontinue therapy. Separation anxiety can appear in many ways. There are few absolutes in therapy, and hopefully both parties realize the merit of flexibility. The therapist should let the patient know that after termination he remains available to the patient and, in fact, will hope to hear from him. If your anxiety about stopping persists, there is a good reason to pause and investigate reasons for this insecurity Perhaps the patient sets a very short separation period hoping to avoid the pain of saying goodbye or because he anticipates the therapist talking him out of his termination plan. The scenarios are endless, but all can be helpfully addressed with sufficient good will, caring, and reason. It might be fitting for your therapist to question your termination plans.

The ending phase of therapy may allow a better understanding of the process of change. A patient in his early 30s came to therapy rather vague about the reasons for his unhappiness. He was a quite capable, intelligent and conscientious fellow. His boss was a relative who ran the company like a dictator, was unreasonably demanding, and intimidating. The boss never had a word of encouragement or praise for his hard working and skilled employee. The patient tolerated the situation for years, unhappy but, in part because of family loyalty, he was unable to become clear about his dissatisfaction with the job and, therefore, unable to extricate himself from the unfortunate situation. It was as though he felt that he deserved no better.

We worked steadily for a long time with my effort being to help him recognize his internal obstacles to evaluating the job. As I got to know him better he revealed other problems parallel to his work. One example was a lack of clarity about not wanting to be with his wife, though he made his unhappiness with the marriage clear to me. Marrying his wife had seemed the expected thing to do. My impression was that he had been trained to accept the status quo, no matter how miserable he might be. Details of his childhood had emerged over several years to confirm this line of reasoning.

When he was five years old, his mother left him and the family. After that, an extremely injured and enraged father would allow no contact between mother and children although mother and children fervently wished to maintain contact. This taboo was extremely painful for the patient and played a significant role in all the children's lives, shaping their expectations as though casting them in concrete. They learned that one must just accept the intolerable. It seemed that for the patient to change he had to do so by allowing an unsatisfactory situation to continue for way too long until reaching a boil when suddenly he would spill the long accumulation of bitter feelings. Following a particularly tumultuous period with his boss, and after many years of unhappiness with him, he suddenly quit, soon acquiring a much better job. After that he had a torrid affair with a woman underscoring how much was missing from his marriage. Some time later he divorced in a kind and considerate manner allowing the couple to remain, on good terms. Then later in an eruptive manner he talked about his dissatisfaction with therapy and, as he saw it, the lack of change. He suddenly, over several sessions, spilled his disappointment and rage about once again accepting an unsatisfactory status quo. Having, for there first time in therapy, and perhaps anywhere, voiced that he had a right to something better, he was able to continue his forward movement until termination. In a brief contact a year later he reported being happily remarried and that he was fulfilling a long held wish to be a father. The couple's child was due in a few months.

H. Some gains from psychotherapy.

The patient and therapist most want to alleviate the patient's symptoms, reduction of pain and suffering. That is usually quite sufficient. But often, in a long-term therapy that is going well there are some qualities and capacities that appear, expand, and provide more protection against a recurrence of severe symptoms

Perhaps most promising is the development of REFLECTIVENESS. The process of inquiry and attention to meaning may lead to a new self-awareness, and capacity to think about motives, feelings, thoughts in a new way, in a positive sense. This involves the ability to think about oneself with perspective and see one's effect on other people, to become aware of the impact of one's behavior. It is a distinctly different state of mind than the unreflective, more impulsive, unknowing way of being that is typical of so many people.

One patient, an accomplished professional, could be callous and unfeeling with other people, sometimes animals. He seemed oblivious to his negative influence. We spent years assembling, and repeating, an understanding of how as a child he felt treated without understanding or recognition of feelings or even that he had feelings. He was repeatedly severely humiliated. His pain was denied and ignored. Along with his progress in a very long therapy he became aware of having done harm, and developed a corresponding reflectiveness together with relatively new sense of remorse, regret, and further, a wish to repair. I was confident in the stability of these changes only after some years.

Next is the growing realization that behavior, thoughts, feelings have MEANING beyond their manifest appearance. As a result of discovering complicated layers of motivation one can feel more appreciation and respect for an internal life. This is a part of increasing self-exploration and the work of understanding unconscious motivation. This kind of change and the one above usually result in markedly improved relationships. One patient who tended to feel empty experienced a shift toward feeling more substance as a result of discovering rich layers of meaning in his dreams. He discovered that he was much more complicated than he previously thought. Over the years a number of patients gained a first sense of their unconscious through our work on the meaning of their dreams.

Another gain may an increased appreciation of the humanness of oneself and the other, the reality of being a feeling person and that others feel, a capacity called EMPATHY. As a patient examines their pain and becomes aware that what one does and says has an impact on others, positive or negative, the result is empathy. Increased empathy is another capacity that allows marked improvement in relationships. Empathy may seem related to sympathy bit is not the same. Sympathy implies feeling sorry "for" rather than "with" the individual. The benefits of therapy are impressively underscored when we can experience that it brings about increased capacity for empathy. The result is a change in that person's character.

There is, of course, no guarantee that therapy will have these positive outcomes. There are patients who seem to not experience gains at all and others for whom gains are not evident until after the conclusion of the therapy. I have worked with patients who seem not to have progressed who write or visit with me years later to tell me how much they learned.

Some people use therapy in an episodic way, gaining a bit from each effort. So if you use therapy every once in a while you might consider that there may be a gradually cumulative effect.

Other patients manifest a reaction to therapy referred to as a "negative therapeutic reaction" and seem to get worse rather than better. They may seem to feel worse every day in every way, a Humpty-Dumpty scenario. Others may experience them as difficult, as having a multitude of complaints while not benefiting from anyone's attempts to help. They tend to be a so-called "help rejecting complainer". You may understand how some therapists confronted with such a person may feel deskilled or demoralized. Both parties are helped by realizing that the patient who induces such demoralization is engaged in a continued test of the therapist's sturdiness and integrity. Perhaps a major problem in their young years was that they had quite fragile parents who had little or no tolerance for their child's needs. The child learned that strength was illusory and that they must repeatedly test that appearance of strength. This stance may be a necessary experience for some patients because, as the negativity is slowly worked through and the therapist neither retaliates or is unduly defensive, the patient may be able to resolve a major problem in living. The key to your improvement in such unhappy circumstances is your perseverance through those stormy and discouraging conditions. Doing this therapy calls for the therapist's ability to recognize potential positive attributes and forward steps in the patient which are not yet clearly identifiable.

I hear of many who claim that therapy allowed them to succeed in a marriage or profession, increased their self-esteem, generosity, and kindness and for a significant number saved their lives. Some were helped to come to terms with something or someone forever lost. Therapy does not promise happiness but should help us to deal with our limitations and wholeheartedly celebrate our triumphs. Of curse I also hear of patients who are critical of their therapy and did not feel helped. Hopefully the therapist and patient gets an opportunity to review the therapy process to explore the role each played in a disappointing outcome.

Chapter 5

HIDDEN INFLUENCES

This Chapter in four parts describes factors that play mostly invisible roles in significantly influencing psychotherapy. These factors may be discussed in therapy if they arise by accident but mostly they are in the background exerting an influence, sometimes pervasive and quiet, like the air we breathe. You could have years of therapy with never a word about them. So what are these mysterious forces?

A. The issue of research support

Therapists may quote research to bolster a case for the effectiveness of their particular approach. There is nothing wrong with referring to research findings during the process of therapy. I may, on a rare occasion, mention studies demonstrating how unconscious ideas may influence us. However, there are uses of research that may not be useful. I am thinking in particular of therapies referred to as "Evidence-based". Of course building into the name of a therapy claim of being based on "evidence" is presumptive. Does that imply that other therapies are not supported by evidence? Further, at least one study examined claims better results of evidence-based therapy compared to so-called psychoanalytic psychotherapy (Shedler, 2015). Not so! Their analytic therapists were graduate students who by training are not close to a reasonable definition of psychoanalytic therapists. Research evidence to be considered as something approaching fact must be replicated. So beware of the message of therapists who claim research results bolster the validity of their approach over others.

For patients to be discouraged, in whatever manner, from challenging the efficacy of therapy is destructive to the therapy process. I have talked with representatives of insurance companies who enthusiastically grasp studies, no matter how shoddy in methodology, that seem to support the effectiveness of short duration therapies, therapies which require little training, and one size fits all approaches.

B. Patterns of reimbursement

In the role of patient, you are unlikely to be unaware of the constraints insurance places on your therapy. My hope is that a more aware consumer may eventually lead to changes in the system. When you begin therapy, if like most people you must use your insurance' you will be assigned a one or two-word diagnostic label by your therapist because he is required to do so by your insurance company. These diagnostic labels are drawn from the Diagnostic and Statistical Manual of Mental Disorders of the American Psychiatric Association. You might ask your therapist what label he assigned to you. The label might be "generalized anxiety disorder"," major depression", "bipolar disorder", among many other possibilities. Some therapists will attach the labels in a perfunctory, haphazard way. They may not think about accuracy, may believe it is a meaningless requirement or use the label that may be least likely to stigmatize or most liable to be granted reimbursement. Because the labels appear in the official APA manual is not evidence of their validity. A collaborative effort of several professional organizations presents a far more psychologically sensitive classification system (PDM Task Force. 2006). However, this new diagnostic system is not widely accepted. So much for the idea that political forces do not play out in the arena of psychotherapy. At the outset let us understand that diagnosis should not be mechanistic or dehumanizing and therefore should consist of much more than labels (Peebles-Kleiger.2002).

Due in part to the constraints imposed by insurance, which will not reimburse for thorough diagnostic studies, such work is, unfortunately, becoming a lost art. The gradual loss of the detailed diagnostic process is significant for those who plan and conduct treatment, particularly a long-term treatment. As the opportunity for that work fades, fewer clinicians possess the skills required and, therefore, don't realize the magnitude of the loss. You can't miss what you don't know. Also, diagnostic understanding based on a team approach (psychiatrist, psychologist, social worker, nurse all working together) may be superior to any one person's assessment. But again insurance will not reimburse for team meeting time, so the multidisciplinary approach also dwindles. Newly trained people may be oblivious to the use of an extended diagnostic process because they may not have been exposed to it and don't know what they are missing.

Perhaps the most serious negative consequence of our insurance system is that it discourages more than one therapy session a week. So therapists are pressured to do no more than once a week psychotherapy, regardless of what they think the frequency should be. For many patients once a week sessions or less is quite suitable. But for many others the result of insurance pressures is that clinicians and patients may accept that once a week is a standard of care. It is not! My preference and that of many other therapists is to conduct twice a week sessions with the majority of the patients, in part because of difficulty maintaining continuity and achieving depth with less. Frequently an insurance program is chosen by the place of employment, and you may not know about limitations before the insurance is purchased. So it is a good idea to inquire about the details of your coverage as soon as possible though it may be that your inquiry will not reveal the insurance limitations. And the limitations may not appear in print. The limitation imposed by insurance is one of multiple factors encouraging briefer and more superficial psychotherapy.

C. Neuroscience and psychiatry

These days we are witnessing an explosion of fascinating neuroscience research facilitated by new imaging technology. I will not go into details about new knowledge of cortical functioning, and I am not well versed in that area. One example of recent learning about the brain studies have shown that the brain of a person who observes another's activity mimics that person's brain activity by way of what is quite speculatively called "mirror neurons." So the question has been posed if we have found a neurological substrate for the mental activity of empathy(Cosolino, 2002). Also, recent studies strongly suggest that early trauma affects brain functioning that, in turn further affects the consequences of trauma, a kind of self-reinforcing cycle. The overstimulation that is part of trauma may permanently produce cortical hyperarousal, resulting in someone who is quick to startle, hypersensitive, hyperalert, too fast to react to all kinds of happenings. As trauma affects brain functioning, it is no wonder that such conditions as PTSD are slow to change. Because such a person is primed to act before thinking they will be even more vulnerable to repeated traumatization. Some good news is that it is likely that long-term psychotherapy will produce brain changes as well, but of the sort that accompany calming.

Accompanying the expansion of neuroscience, some people may believe that everything psychological can ultimately be explained by biology, referred to by a colleague as "bio-mania". However, it is unlikely that human subjectivity, meaning, and motivation will ever translate into physical explanations. In the meantime, an enormous amount of financial resources are being poured into biological research as compared to the paucity of funds devoted to the study of psychotherapy.

In the field of psychiatry, scientific appearances, including research on the brain and medications, have come to distract attention from therapy so that psychotherapy plays less and less a role in training and practice. Sadly, it is increasingly rare to find psychoanalytically informed psychiatrists, to which any of us involved in the training of psychiatric residents can testify. Why is this a major concern? One reason is that patients in psychotherapy must rely for medication on people who will not understand their psychotherapy experience. Of even greater concern, the psychiatrist's office is the entry point into treatment of an enormous number of patients who will be told that medication is superior to therapy rather than the fact that the two modalities compliment one another.

Attention Deficit Disorder (ADD)is a condition that tends to be underdiagnosed and for which the helpfulness of therapy is underestimated. Before dismissing that the possibility that you may have features of the disorder you might complete one of the many ADD symptom checklists online or in print in ADD self-help books. These simple inventories ask about your ability to maintain focus and attention, memory, and assess hyperarousal, restlessness, including behaviors like being unable to sit still for long or being chronically late. ADD can create or exacerbate relationship problems, and it can interfere with your use of therapy. For example, it is likely that you will have difficulty remembering sessions. Or you may frequently interrupt your therapist because any delay may result in your loosing track of what you wanted to say. Often overlooked is that in addition to the brain based contributions the patient must deal with the impact on self-image and self-esteem of years of ADD problems including problematic self-regulation. Starting early the ADD child has likely been told that he is lazy, if he just tried harder he would do better, he is stupid, is bright but a slacker and is a troublemaker. And the patient may be bewildered that so much effort is required for tasks that are relatively easy for others. The ADD patient may discover some upside consisting, for example, in enhanced creative abilities and other tasks where moving quickly can be an asset.

D. Issues In Diagnosis

Earlier I discussed a simplified label oriented use of diagnosis. But we are better off viewing diagnosis as a nuanced, comprehensive understanding. Including values and ambitions, strengths, vulnerabilities, thought style preferred defenses, responses to stress, relationship patterns and internal factors that help or harm one's ability to live a good life. Some therapists claim that any diagnostic label or even more extensive diagnostic studies, because a caricature, do more harm than good. For myself I can not see how knowledge about patients, from whatever source, should be discarded. Whether you consider the reference to labels useful or not chances are that classifications are here to stay. So it is incumbent upon us to be as aware of them and their implications as we can. By way of illustration, we reviewed above some issues relevant to proper treatment that follow from a diagnosis of ADD.

It is useful for the therapist to share understanding of the patient as it evolves, with or without labels. Even when a thorough initial diagnostic evaluation is conducted, the information should be shared with the patient, with all due consideration for timing and tact. You should know a fact not available to most patients, that a formal diagnostic evaluation is only as good as the training and skill of the examiner. You may have reason to question the thoroughness and depth of paper and pencil assessments. Ideally a diagnostic understanding should evolve for both patient and therapist over the course of your work together and thereby become part of the therapy.

I will, briefly describe a few of the most commonly used diagnostic categories, most importantly with the implications spelled out. First I will discuss hysteria as a diagnosis not because it is an "official" label, but rather because it is so prominent in the development of psychoanalytic history and has become common in everyday parlance. The person described as a hysteric relies on the defenses of repression and denial. Consequently, as mentioned in my earlier discussion of defenses, they cut themselves off from threatening parts of their internal world, resulting in gaps in their understanding of themselves and others. The person may seem naive or oblivious. Their thought style is global, impressionistic, imprecise tending to avoid detail and tasks calling for precision. Their symptoms tend to be saturated with symbolic meaning representing forbidden thoughts or wishes. For example, a person who suffers from agoraphobia may be unconsciously showing that they fear independent functioning. If you can't leave your home you can't seperate. When I was planning a trip out of town, a client dreamed that my legs were cut off. As we discussed the dream, we discovered his wish that I do not leave him. Well functioning hysterics may excel in the arts, theater, and other performance skills and activities with flare. The obsessive-compulsive person uses thinking to ward off troubling emotions while the hysteric uses a show of emotion to block out disturbing thoughts.

The person labeled bipolar thinks in polarities (Good vs. bad, right vs. wrong) rather than gradations, consequently viewing life in extremes. Those extremes appear in moods manifested in agitated states of mania in which the person feels invulnerable and then profoundly dark, unrelenting depression. Often at the extremes of this condition people need highly structured treatment to supplement their therapy. However, residential programs that will invest the time to treat more troubled people long-term are now hard to find. When well-functioning the bipolar individual may seem merely moody, driven, ambitious, and emotionally variable.

I will discuss narcissism (or narcissistic defenses) a bit longer than other labels because it is used so often, and incorrectly, in everyday parlance. This label may be more applicable than any other for people in the modern world. People labeled "narcissistic personality disorder" are often unable to experience love. Relationships are viewed as either exploitive or manipulative. They can be demeaning and to blatantly place their needs ahead of others. They may be good at identifying other's needs when to do so helps them further their interests. They may exaggerate their feelings, achievements and sometimes even their miseries. What is not so easy to recognize is that usually they are unhappy, perhaps covered by a glossy superficiality or self-inflation, with a less visible profound sense of emptiness. These difficulties tend to originate when parents treat their child as an extension of themselves, oblivious to the child's real needs. The person with a healthy sense of narcissism is more sure of his self-worth, perhaps with a bit of exaggeration. The need to be special and to have an inflated self-image works well for many people who may turn out to be good actors, good self-marketers, captains of industry, prominent politicians and may excel in other activities requiring skills in self-promotion. When psychotherapy is going well for a time this group tends to become somewhat depressed. The therapy work on their narcissistic defences of denial and omnipotence may leave them feeling psychologically naked.

The patient labeled borderline poses some characteristic problems for their therapists. They tend to be emotionally volatile, unpredictable, and to polarize, dividing the world into good and bad, positions that can quickly shift. Their sense of self and others is uncertain and fluid. For this troubled person, a slight or rejection may result in storms of emotion and difficulty modulating their responses. Some clinicians have identified flawed self-regulation as the primary source of trouble. As children, even as babies, they were hard to soothe and comfort. During storms of emotion, reason may be swept aside with resulting highly irrational impulsive behavior.

Therapists agree that many patients in the borderline category seem constitutionally predisposed to develop their disturbance and that they suffered from severe early trauma, as in severe neglect or abuse. Perhaps therapy with these patients should be reserved for the most skilled and experienced therapists, by no means assured. Therapists may avoid taking the borderline patient into therapy because of not wanting to deal with frequent crises, need for additional sessions, frequent phone calls and tensions produced by self-destructive behavior. However, patients and therapists willing to ride out the storms of emotion and action, sometimes for many years, may eventually be rewarded by significant improvement in the patient's life.

An occasional problem with diagnostic thinking is that the patient may respond to that scrutiny by feeling dehumanized, under a microscope. If the two parties to therapy can achieve an understanding of the patient together, we model partnership. The patient may have a sense of being better understood than at any prior time in their life, therapeutic in itself. Borderline patients might also achieve some success in life in their idiosyncratic and rather tumultuous way.

Before leaving the subject of diagnosis, attention deserves to be devoted to physical factors. Near the beginning of therapy, I usually ask the patient to have a physical exam. Psychological and emotional problems can be caused or exacerbated by physical conditions. I was working with a patient who became agitated and unreasonable, seemingly out of the blue. A big part of the problem was that he had been inadvertently prescribed two different but equally powerful stimulants. The results were that he suffered a highly agitated state of mind accompanied by impulsivity, agitation, and irrational near delusional thinking. Another patient came to me because of with recurrent severe headaches. Based on a hunch I referred him to a neurologist who discovered a brain tumor. You can be surer of the psychological causes of symptoms when physical factors have been ruled out.

SUMMARY AND CONCLUSIONS

My primary intent has been to explain for psychotherapy patients how therapy works, its benefits, how it may be affected by personality styles, vulnerabilities and external influences (like insurance). I wish to make therapy more "user friendly" and to some extent to demystify the process. My dreams for the book are that there be a copy in therapist's waiting rooms, that it be included in introductory courses for students and trainees, and be easily available for all those wishing to better understand therapy. In Chapter I reviews the various reasons people seek therapy and how they may go about finding a therapist well suited to their needs. Then Chapter 2 reviews some concepts that help to understand psychotherapy and our psychological functioning, namely the role of relationships in forming us, including our patterns of attachment to others, the part played by unconscious processes, defenses and boundaries. I dwell on the crucial importance in many therapies of work on transference and countertransference and provide clinical examples. Chapter 3 focuses on the symptoms that cause us to seek therapy. In order to understand symptoms it is useful to recognize that they have meaning. A primary task in therapy is to search for those meanings, make them conscious, and subject to modification. Chapter 4 describes stages of therapy, the beginning, middle and end. Here we look at how the therapist thinks, why he behaves in certain ways and specifically how he facilitates the therapy. In Chapter 5 I outline how some forces seemingly independent of therapy, in fact mostly unconsciously, exert a powerful influence on the process of therapy.

REFERENCES

1. Ainsworth, M.D.S. Blehar, M.C., Waters, E. & Wall, S (1978). Patterns of attachment: A psychological study of the stranger situation, Hillsdale, New Jersey

2. Allen, J.G.(1998) Coping With Trauma: A guide to self-understanding. Washington, D.C: American Psychiatric Press.

3. Allen, J.G. (2006) Mentalizing in Practice. In Handbook of Mentalization Based Treatments eds J.G. Allen and P. Fonagy. Hoboken, N.J., Wiley, pp 3-30.

4. Allen J.G.(2001) Traumatic Relationships and serious mental disorders. New York. J wiley & Sons.

5. Beebe, B, Lachman, F.M.(2002) Infant Research and Adult Treatment: Co-constructing Interactions. Hillsdale, N.J.The Analytic Press

6. Benjamin, Jessica.(1998) Shadow of the other: Intersubjectivity and gender in psychoanalysis. New York: Rutledge

7. Bollas, C. (1987). The Shadow of The Object, New York, Columbia University Press.

8. Colson, D.B.(1995) An Analysts Multiple Losses: Countertransference and other reactions. Contemporary Psychoanalysis, Vol 31, No. 3. 459-478

9. Colson, D.B. (1982).: Protectiveness in borderline patients: a neglected object relations paradigm. Topeka, Ks., Bull, Menninger Clinic 46:305-320

10. Colson D.B., Horwitz L, Allen JG, et al(1988) Patient collaboration as a criterion for the therapeutic alliance. Psychoanalytic Psychology 5: 259-269

11. Cozolino, L.(2002) The Neuroscience of Psychotherapy: Building and Rebuilding the Human Brain. Norton, NY. 20027

12. Fonagy, P.,Gergely, G., Jurist, E., 8. Target, M.(2002) Affect regulation, mentalization and the development of the self. New York, Other Press.

13. Friedman. RA. (2007)Psychiatry's Identity Crisis. The New York Times Sunday Review.

14. Guntrip, H (1971). Psychoanalytic Theory, Therapy and The Self, New York, Basic Books

15. Greenberg, J.(2015) Disappointment: Something in the nature of analysis. Journal of The American Psychoanalytic Association Vol. 63, No. 6, 1215-1223

16. Horwitz, L. (2104)Listening With The Fourth Ear: Unconscious Dynamics in Analytic Group Psychotherapy.(2014) London, Karmac,

17. Horwitz, L., Gabbard, G.O., Allen, Jon G., Frieswyk, S.H., Colson, D.B., Newsom, G.E, Coyne, L.(2005) Borderline Personality Disorder: Tailoring the Psychotherapy to The Patient. American Psychiatric Press. Washington, D.C.

18. Leichsenning, F., Abbass, A., Luyten, P., Hilsenroth, M., Rabung, S. (2013) The emerging evidence for long-term psychodynamic therapy. Psychodynamic Psychiatry., 42,(3), 381-384

19. Lichtenberg, J.(2005) Craft and Spirit: A guide to the exploratory therapies. Hillsdale, N.J. The Analytic Press.

20. McWilliams, N. (2004). Psychoanalytic Psychotherapy: A Practitioner's Guide. New York The Guilford Press

21. Mitchell, S.A.(2000) Relationality: From Attachment to Intersubjectivity Hillsdale, N.J. The Analytic Press, Hillsdale, N.J

22. Peebles-Kleiger, Mary Jo.(2002) Beginnings: The Art and Science of Planning Psychotherapy. Hillsdale, N.J. The Analytic Press,

23. Person, E.,Cooper, A., Gabbard, G. (Eds)(2005) Textbook of psychoanalysis. Washington, D.C. American Psychiatric Publishing, Inc., p. 561.

24. PDM Task Force (2006). Psychodynamic Diagnostic Manual. Silver Spring, MD: Alliance Of Psychoanalytic Organizations.

25. Seligman, M. (1995) The effectiveness of psychotherapy. The Consumer Reports Study. American Psychologist,50, 965-974.20.

26. Shedler, J.(2010) The efficiency of psychodynamic psychotherapy. The American Psychologist, 65 (2), 98-109

27. Shedler, J.(2015) Where is the evidence for "evidence-based" therapy? The Journal of Psychological Therapies in Primary Care. Vol. 4: pp 47-59

28. Stern, D.(1995) The Motherhood Constellation: A Unified View of Parent-Infant Psychotherapy. Basic Books.

29. Stolorow, R.D.(1992) The Intersubjective Foundations of Psychological Life. Hillsdale, N.J.The Analytic Press

30. Target, M. (2002) Affect regulation, mentalization and the development of the self. New York, Other Press.

31. Wallerstein, R.S.(1986) Forty-two Lives In Treatment: A study of Psychoanalysis and Psychotherapy. New York, Guilford

32. Yalom, I. D.(2009) The Gift of Therapy: An open letter to a new generation of therapists and their patients. New York. Harper